W9-ANB-303

THE EASY FAKE BOOK

Melody, Lyrics, and Simplified Chords

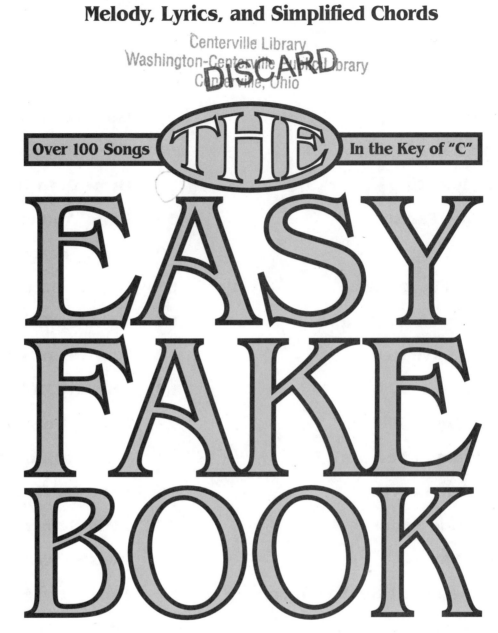

Over 100 Songs · THE · In the Key of "C"

EASY FAKE BOOK

ISBN 0-634-00905-2

HAL•LEONARD® CORPORATION

7777 W. BLUEMOUND RD. P.O. BOX 13819 MILWAUKEE, WI 53213

Visit Hal Leonard Online at
www.halleonard.com

"C" Edition

THE EASY FAKE BOOK

CONTENTS

5	Alfie		52	God Bless' the Child
7	All I Ask of You		54	Great Balls of Fire
10	All My Loving		56	Grow Old with Me
12	Almost Paradise		58	Hello, Young Lovers
11	Always		60	Here, There and Everywhere
14	Always in My Heart		62	Hey, Good Lookin'
16	Always on My Mind		64	How Are Things in Glocca Morra
18	And I Love Her		66	How Deep Is Your Love
20	Angel		68	I Believe in You and Me
26	Any Dream Will Do		72	I Can't Get Started with You
24	Autumn in New York		74	I Didn't Know What Time It Was
23	Autumn Leaves		76	I Left My Heart in San Francisco
28	The Blue Room		78	I Will Remember You
30	Blue Skies		80	I Wish I Were in Love Again
32	By the Time I Get to Phoenix		82	I Write the Songs
34	Cabaret		84	I'll Be Seeing You
36	Call Me Irresponsible		94	I'll Be There
38	(They Long to Be) Close to You		86	I've Got the World on a String
40	Crazy		88	If
42	Do Nothin' Till You Hear from Me		90	Imagine
44	Fields of Gold		92	In a Sentimental Mood
46	The First Time Ever I Saw Your Face		97	In the Wee Small Hours of the Morning
48	The Glory of Love		71	It Could Happen to You
50	Go the Distance		98	It Might As Well Be Spring

100	It Never Entered My Mind
102	Jailhouse Rock
104	Kansas City
106	The Lady Is a Tramp
110	Lazy River
108	Love Me with All Your Heart
112	Makin' Whoopee!
114	Memories of You
116	Memory
118	Michelle
111	Misty
120	Mona Lisa
122	Moon River
124	Moonlight in Vermont
128	My Girl
126	My Heart Will Go On (Love Theme from 'Titanic')
131	(You Make Me Feel Like) A Natural Woman
134	The Nearness of You
136	A Nightingale Sang in Berkeley Square
138	One Less Bell to Answer
140	People
142	Release Me
144	Rockin' Chair
159	Save the Best for Last
146	Skylark
148	Solitude
150	Some Enchanted Evening
152	Somebody Loves Me
154	Something
156	Sometimes When We Touch
162	Sophisticated Lady
164	Stand by Me
166	Star Dust
168	Stella by Starlight
170	Tangerine
172	Tears in Heaven
176	Tennessee Waltz
178	There's a Small Hotel
175	This Can't Be Love
180	Unchained Melody
182	Valentine
184	The Very Thought of You
186	Walkin' After Midnight
188	The Way We Were
190	What a Wonderful World
192	What'll I Do?
194	What's New?
196	Where the Boys Are
198	Will You Love Me Tomorrow
193	With a Song in My Heart
200	You Took Advantage of Me
204	You've Got a Friend
202	Your Cheatin' Heart
207	Chord Speller

INTRODUCTION

What Is a Fake Book?

A fake book has one-line music notation consisting of melody, lyrics and chord symbols. This lead sheet format is a "musical shorthand" which is an invaluable resource for all musicians—hobbyists to professionals.

Here's how *The Easy Fake Book* differs from most standard fake books:

- All songs are in the key of C.

- Many of the melodies have been simplified.

- Only five basic chord types are used—major, minor, seventh, diminished and augmented.

- The music notation is larger for ease of reading.

- Introductions are included to establish the "flavor" of the song.

In the event that you haven't used chord symbols to create accompaniment, or your experience is limited, a chord speller chart is included at the back of the book to help you get started.

Have fun!

ALFIE
Theme from the Paramount Picture ALFIE

Words by HAL DAVID
Music by BURT BACHARACH

What's it all a - bout, Al - fie? _____ Is it
on - ly fools are kind, Al - fie, _____ then I

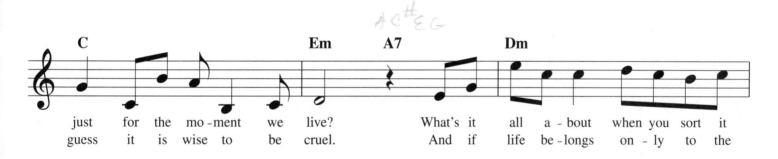

just for the mo - ment we live? What's it all a - bout when you sort it
guess it is wise to be cruel. And if life be - longs on - ly to the

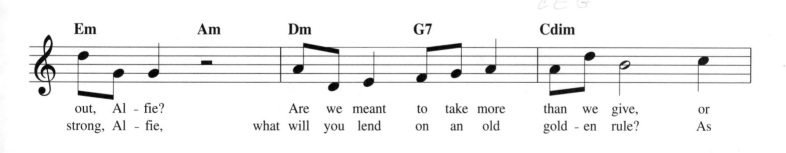

out, Al - fie? Are we meant to take more than we give, or
strong, Al - fie, what will you lend on an old gold - en rule? As

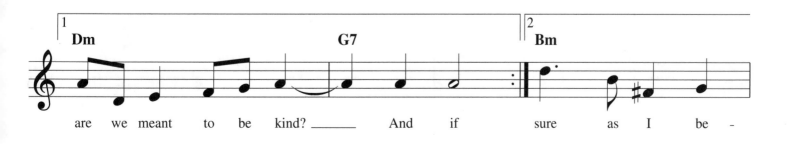

are we meant to be kind? _____ And if sure as I be -

lieve there's a heav-en a - bove Al - fie, I

know there's some-thing much more, some-thing e - ven non - be-liev - ers

can be - lieve in. I be - lieve in love, Al - fie. _____

With -out true love we just ex - ist, Al - fie. Un -til you find the love you've

missed you're noth - ing, Al - fie. When you walk let your heart lead the way, and

you'll find love an -y day, Al - fie, Al - fie.

ALL I ASK OF YOU
from THE PHANTOM OF THE OPERA

Music by ANDREW LLOYD WEBBER
Lyrics by CHARLES HART
Additional Lyrics by RICHARD STILGOE

ALL MY LOVING

from A HARD DAY'S NIGHT

Words and Music by JOHN LENNON
and PAUL McCARTNEY

Close your eyes and I'll kiss you, to-mor-row I'll
tend that I'm kiss-ing the lips I am

miss you; re-mem-ber I'll al-ways be true. _____
miss-ing, and hope that my dreams will come true. _____

_____ And then while I'm a-way, I'll write home ev-'ry

day, _____ and I'll send all my lov-ing to you. _____

1. I'll pre- _____
2. All my lov-ing I will send to you. _____

All my lov-ing, dar-ling I'll be true. _____

ALWAYS

Words and Music by
IRVING BERLIN

ALMOST PARADISE
Love Theme from the Paramount Motion Picture FOOTLOOSE

Words by DEAN PITCHFORD
Music by ERIC CARMEN

I thought that dreams be-longed to oth-er men, 'cause each time I got close they'd fall a-part a-gain.
It seems like per-fect love's so hard to find. I'd al-most giv-en up; you must have read my mind.

I feared my heart would beat in se-cre-cy. I
And all these dreams I saved for a rain-y day, they're

faced the night a-lone, oh, how could I have known that
fi-n'lly com-in' true. I'll share them all with you, 'cause

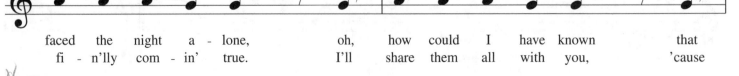

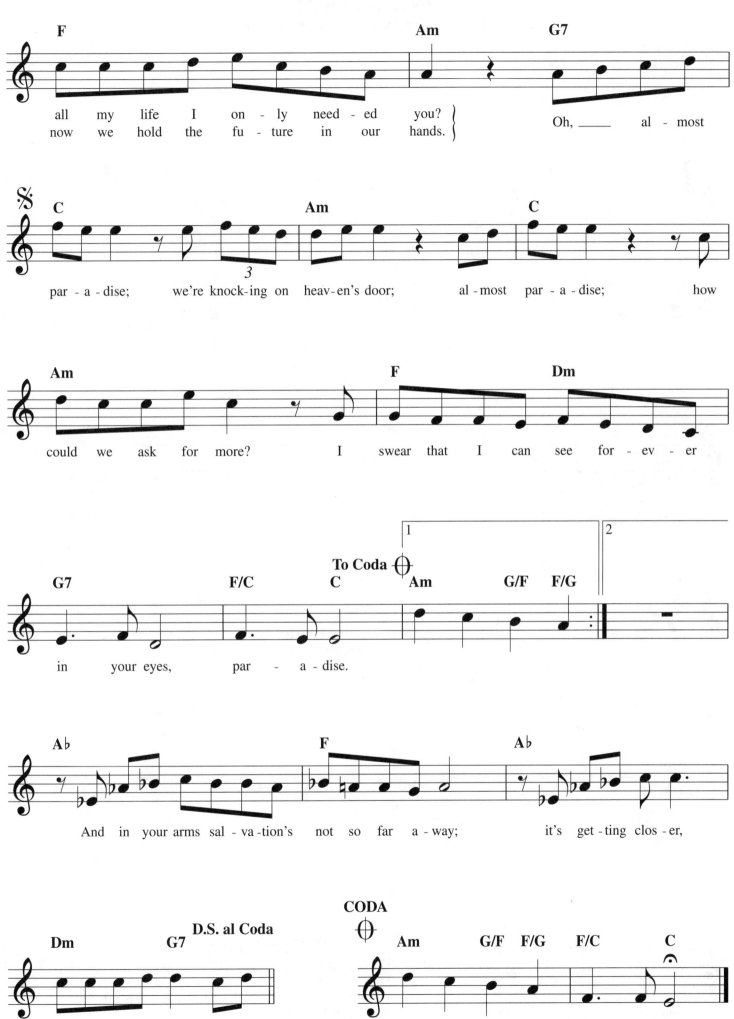

ALWAYS IN MY HEART
(Siempre en mi corazón)

Music and Spanish Words by ERNESTO LECUONA
English Words by KIM GANNON

ALWAYS ON MY MIND

Words and Music by WAYNE THOMPSON,
MARK JAMES and JOHNNY CHRISTOPHER

AND I LOVE HER

Words and Music by JOHN LENNON
and PAUL McCARTNEY

as long as I _____ have you near me. _____

CODA

(Instrumental solo)
Bright as the stars ____ that shine, _ dark is the sky. _

_____ I know this love of mine _ will nev-er die. _

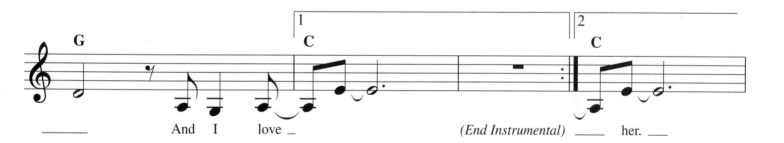

_____ And I love _ *(End Instrumental)* ____ her. ___

(Instrumental)

ANGEL

Words and Music by
SARAH McLACHLAN

rev - er - ie. _____ You're in the arms

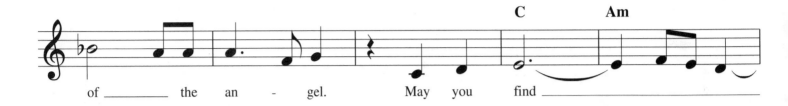

of _____ the an - gel. May you find _____

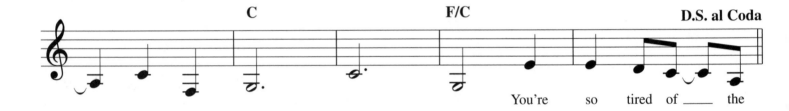

_____ some com - fort _____ here. (Instrumental)

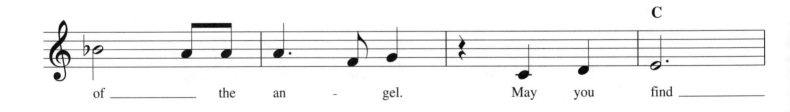

You're so tired of ___ the

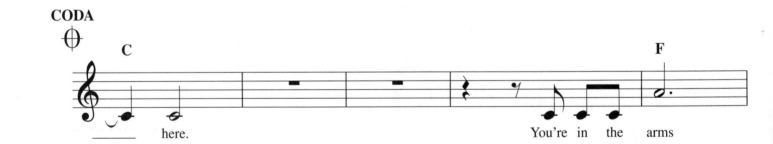

CODA

_____ here. You're in the arms

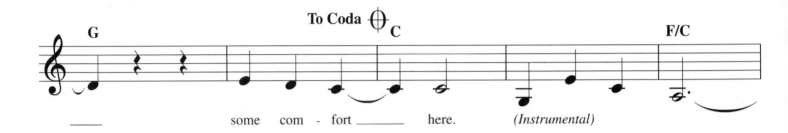

of _____ the an - gel. May you find _____

_____ some com - fort _____ here. _____

AUTUMN LEAVES
(Les Feuilles Mortes)

English lyric by JOHNNY MERCER
French lyric by JACQUES PREVERT
Music by JOSEPH KOSMA

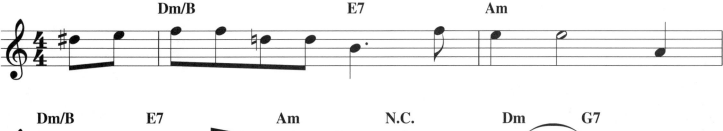

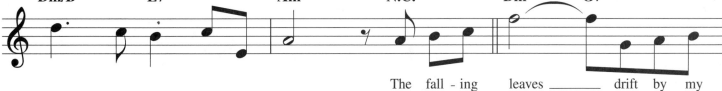

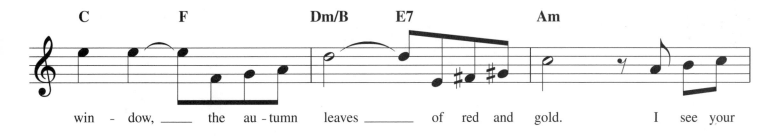

The fall-ing leaves _____ drift by my

win-dow, _____ the au-tumn leaves _____ of red and gold. I see your

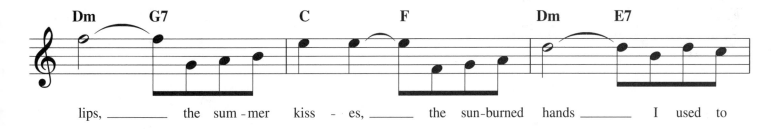

lips, _____ the sum-mer kiss-es, _____ the sun-burned hands _____ I used to

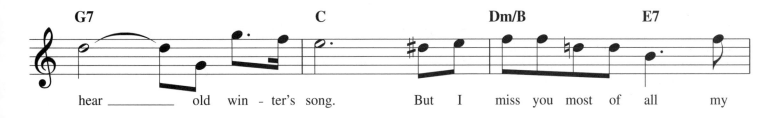

hold. Since you went a-way _____ the days grow long, _____ and soon I'll

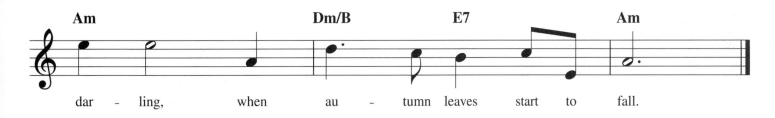

hear _____ old win-ter's song. But I miss you most of all my

dar-ling, when au-tumn leaves start to fall.

AUTUMN IN NEW YORK

Words and Music by
VERNON DUKE

ANY DREAM WILL DO
from JOSEPH AND THE AMAZING TECHNICOLOR DREAMCOAT

Music by ANDREW LLOYD WEBBER
Lyrics by TIM RICE

A crash of drums _ a flash of light, _ my

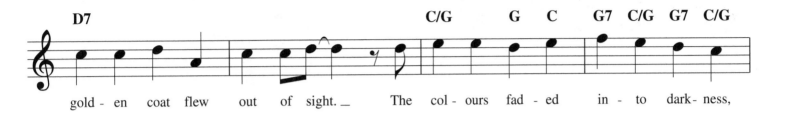

gold - en coat flew out of sight. _ The col - ours fad - ed in - to dark - ness,

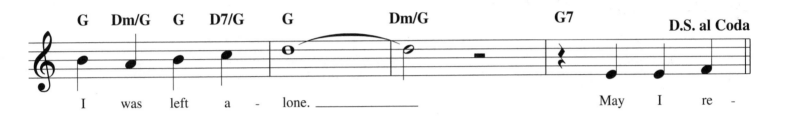

I was left a - lone. _____ May I re -

CODA

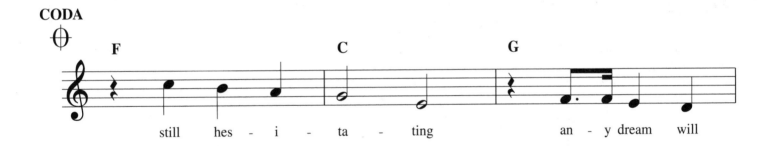

still hes - i - ta - ting an - y dream will

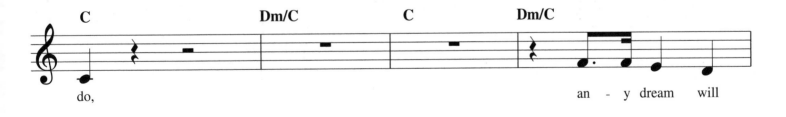

do, an - y dream will

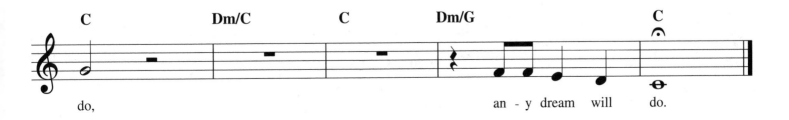

do, an - y dream will do.

THE BLUE ROOM

from THE GIRL FRIEND

Words by LORENZ HART
Music by RICHARD RODGERS

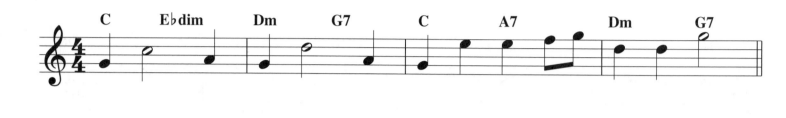

We'll have a blue room, a new room, for two, room, where

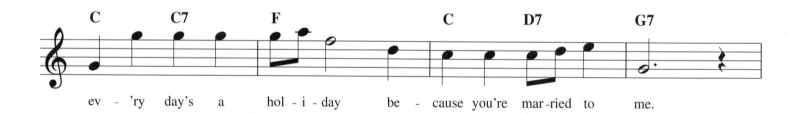

ev - 'ry day's a hol - i - day be - cause you're mar - ried to me.

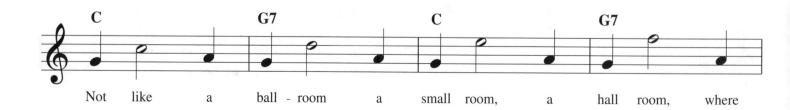

Not like a ball - room a small room, a hall room, where

BLUE SKIES
from BETSY

Words and Music by
IRVING BERLIN

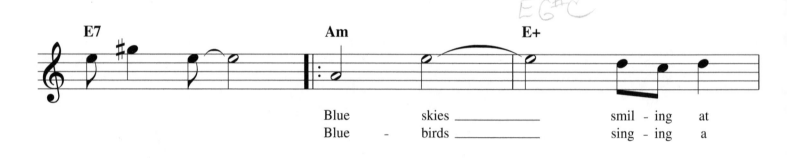

Blue skies _____ smil - ing at
Blue - birds _____ sing - ing a

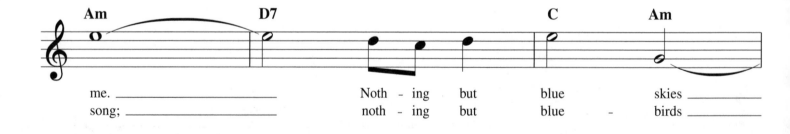

me. _____ Noth - ing but blue skies _____
song; _____ noth - ing but blue - birds _____

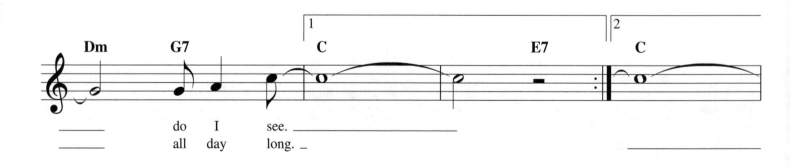

_____ do I see. _____
_____ all day long. _____

BY THE TIME I GET TO PHOENIX

Words and Music by
JIMMY WEBB

By the time _____ I get to Phoe - nix she'll be
time I make Al - bu - quer - que she'll be
time I make Ok - la - ho - ma she'll be

ri - sin', _____ she'll ___ find the note I left
work - in', _____ she'll ___ pro - 'bly stop at
sleep - in', _____ she'll turn soft - ly and

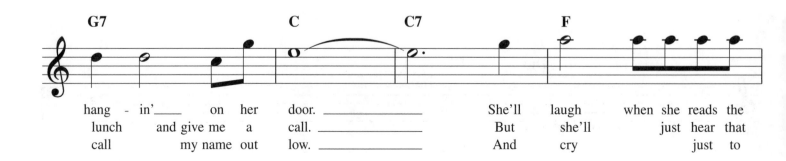

hang - in' ____ on her door. _____ She'll laugh when she reads the
lunch and give me a call. _____ But she'll just hear that
call my name out low. _____ And cry just to

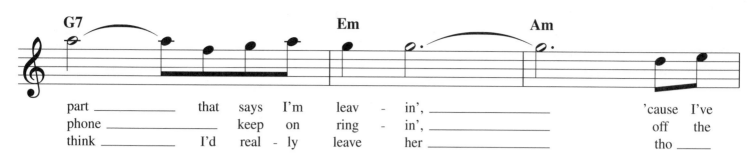

part _____ that says I'm leav - in', _____ 'cause I've
phone _____ keep on ring - in', _____ off the
think _____ I'd real - ly leave her _____ tho ____

left that girl so man - y times be - fore. _____ By the

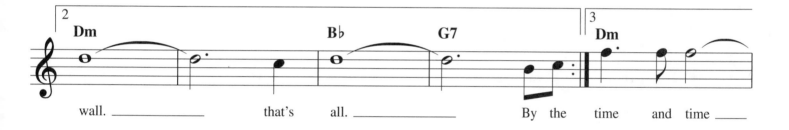

wall. _____ that's all. _____ By the time and time ____

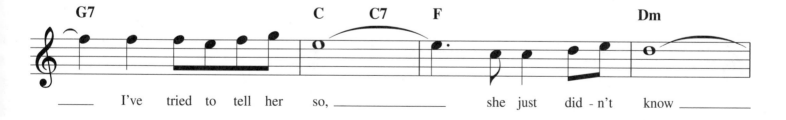

____ I've tried to tell her so, _____ she just did - n't know _____

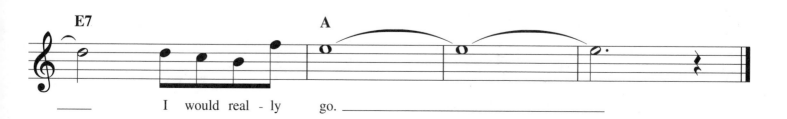

____ I would real - ly go. _____

CABARET
from the Musical CABARET

Words by FRED EBB
Music by JOHN KANDER

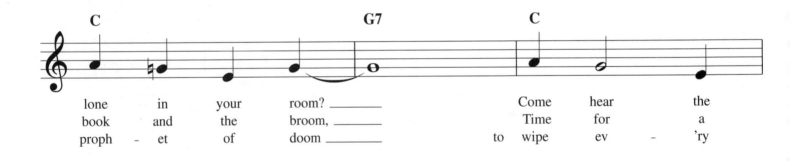

What good is sit-ting a-
Put down the knit-ting the
No use per-mit-ting some

lone in your room? _____ Come hear the
book and the broom, _____ Time for a
proph-et of doom _____ to wipe ev-'ry

mu - sic play. _____
hol - i - day. _____
smile a - way. _____

To Coda ⊕

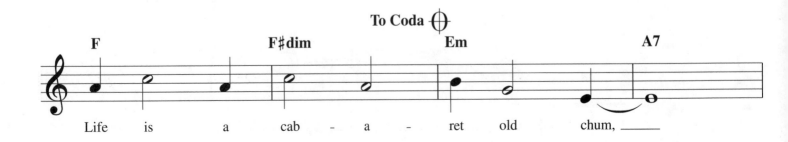

Life is a cab-a-ret old chum, _____

CALL ME IRRESPONSIBLE
from the Paramount Picture PAPA'S DELICATE CONDITION

Words by SAMMY CAHN
Music by JAMES VAN HEUSEN

Call me ir - re - spon - si - ble, call me

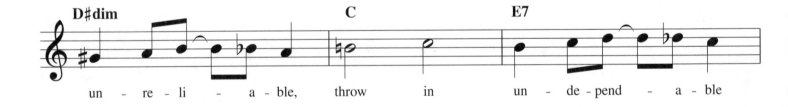

un - re - li - a - ble, throw in un - de - pend - a - ble

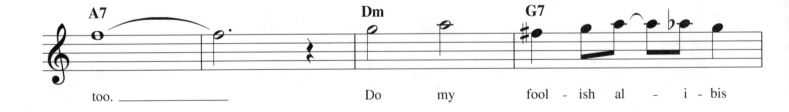

too. _____ Do my fool - ish al - i - bis

bore you? Well, I'm not too clev - er. I

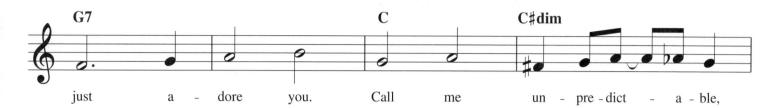

just a - dore you. Call me un - pre - dict - a - ble,

tell me I'm im - prac - ti - cal, rain - bows

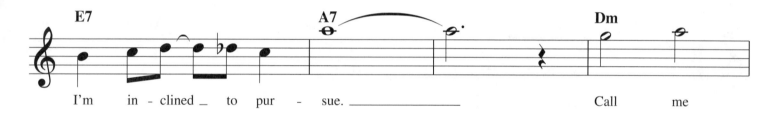

I'm in - clined _ to pur - sue. _____ Call me

ir - re - spon - si - ble, yes, I'm un - re - li - a - ble,

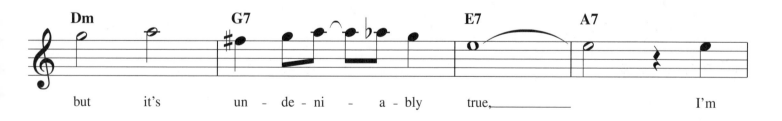

but it's un - de - ni - a - bly true,_____ I'm

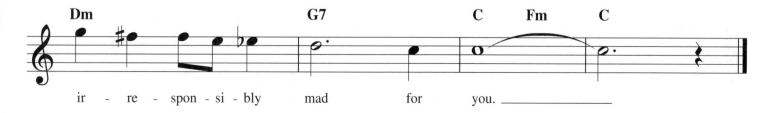

ir - re - spon - si - bly mad for you. _____

(THEY LONG TO BE) CLOSE TO YOU

Lyric by HAL DAVID
Music by BURT BACHARACH

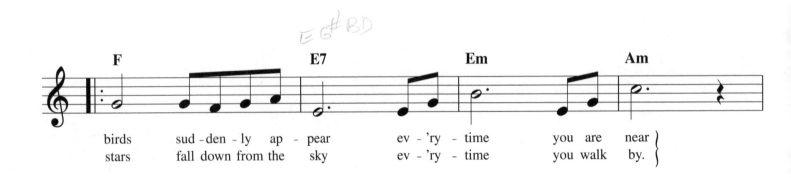

birds   sud - den - ly   ap - pear   ev - 'ry - time   you are   near
stars   fall down from the   sky   ev - 'ry - time   you walk   by.

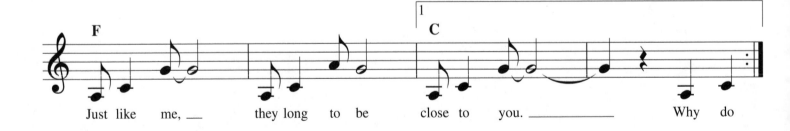

Just like   me, __   they long   to   be   close to   you. ___   Why do

close to   you. ___   On the   day   that you   were born   the

ACᵗEC

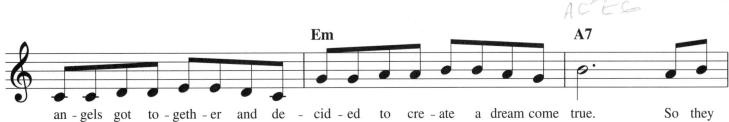

an-gels got to-geth-er and de-cid-ed to cre-ate a dream come true. So they

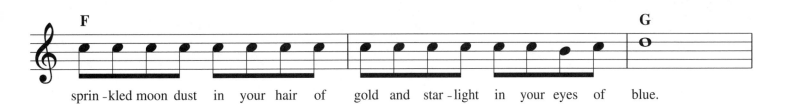

sprin-kled moon dust in your hair of gold and star-light in your eyes of blue.

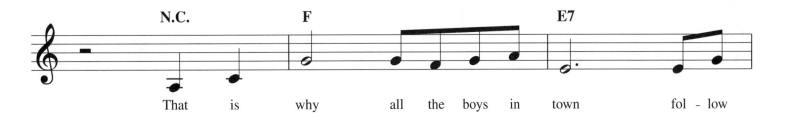

That is why all the boys in town fol-low

you all a-round. Just like me, _____

they long to be close to you. _____ close to you. _____

CRAZY

Words and Music by
WILLIE NELSON

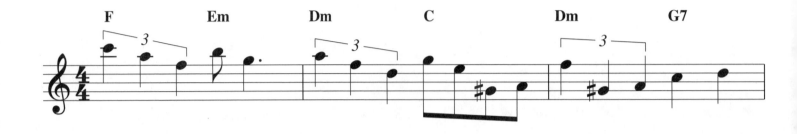

Cra - zy, _____ cra - zy for feel - in' so

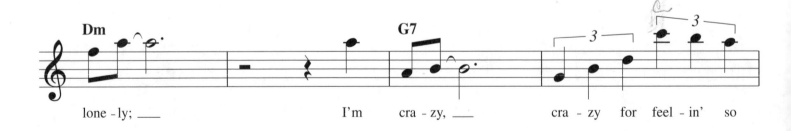

lone - ly; _____ I'm cra - zy, _____ cra - zy for feel - in' so

blue. I knew _____ you'd love me as long as you

DO NOTHIN' TILL YOU HEAR FROM ME

Words and Music by BOB RUSSELL
and DUKE ELLINGTON

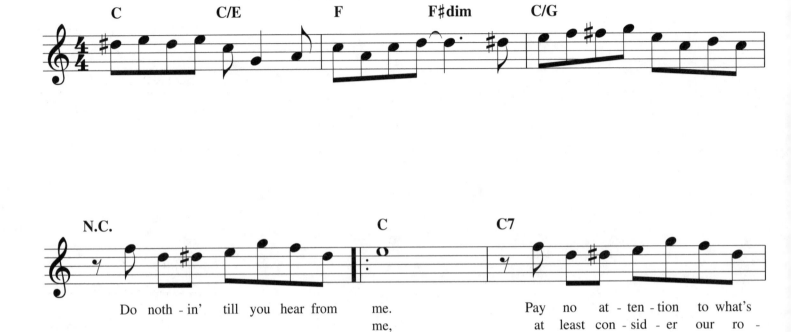

Do noth-in' till you hear from me.
me,

Pay no at-ten-tion to what's
at least con-sid-er our ro-

said,
mance;

why peo-ple tear the seam of an-y-one's dream
if you should take the word of oth-ers you've heard

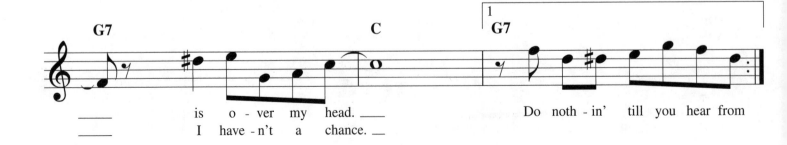

_____ is o-ver my head. ____
_____ I have-n't a chance. ___

Do noth-in' till you hear from

FIELDS OF GOLD

Written and Composed by
STING

(Instrumental)

THE FIRST TIME EVER I SAW YOUR FACE

Words and Music by
EWAN MacCOLL

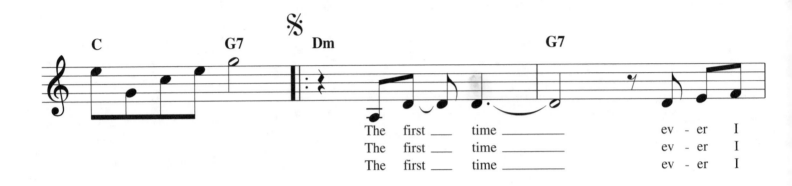

The first ____ time _____ ev - er I
The first ____ time _____ ev - er I
The first ____ time _____ ev - er I

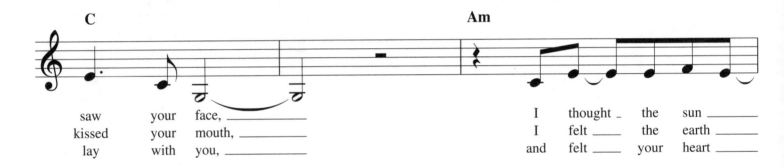

saw   your   face, _____   I   thought ___ the   sun _____
kissed your   mouth, _____   I   felt ____ the   earth _____
lay   with   you, _____   and felt ____ your   heart _____

____   rose   in your eyes. _____   And the moon __
____   move   in my hand. _____   Like the trem -
____   so   close to   mine. _____   And I knew __

To Coda ⊕

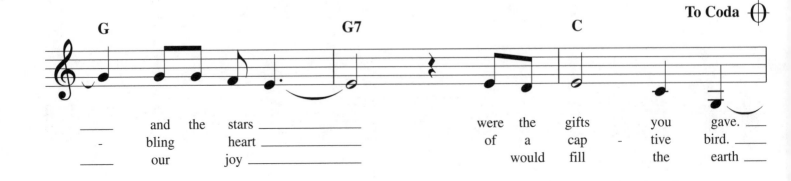

_____   and   the   stars _____   were   the   gifts   you   gave. __
-   bling   heart _____   of   a   cap - tive   bird. __
_____   our   joy _____   would   fill   the   earth __

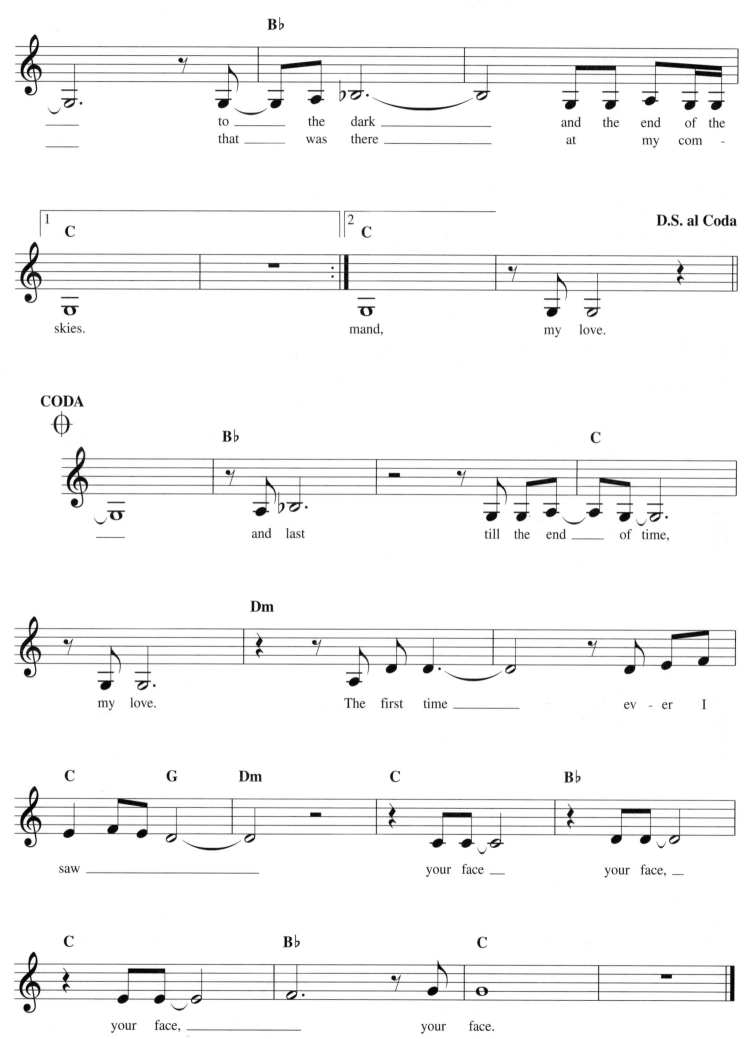

THE GLORY OF LOVE

Words and Music by
BILLY HILL

You've got to give a lit - tle, take a lit - tle
laugh a lit - tle, cry a lit - tle

and let your poor heart break a lit - tle;
be - fore the clouds roll by a lit - tle;

that's the sto - ry of,

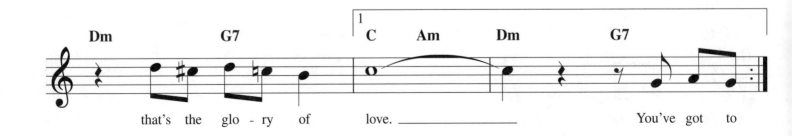

that's the glo - ry of love. _____ You've got to

GO THE DISTANCE
from Walt Disney Pictures' HERCULES

Music by ALAN MENKEN
Lyrics by DAVID ZIPPEL

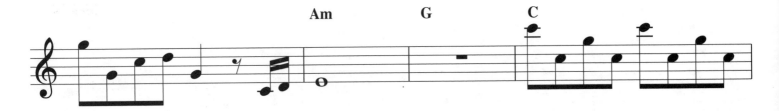

I have of-ten dreamed of a far-off place where a

great warm wel-come will be wait-ing for me. Where the crowds will cheer when they

see my face, and a voice keeps say-ing this is where I'm meant to

be. _____ I will find my way. I can go the dis-tance. I'll be

GOD BLESS' THE CHILD

Words and Music by ARTHUR HERZOG JR.
and BILLIE HOLIDAY

GREAT BALLS OF FIRE

Words and Music by OTIS BLACKWELL
and JACK HAMMER

You shake my nerves and you rat-tle my brain. __ Too much love drives a man in-sane. __

You broke my will, but what a thrill. Good-ness gra-cious, great __ balls of fire!

I laughed at love 'cause I thought it was fun-ny. You came a-long and you moved __ me, hon-ey. I changed my mind,

love's just fine. __ Good-ness gra-cious, great __ balls of fire!

GROW OLD WITH ME

Words and Music by
JOHN LENNON

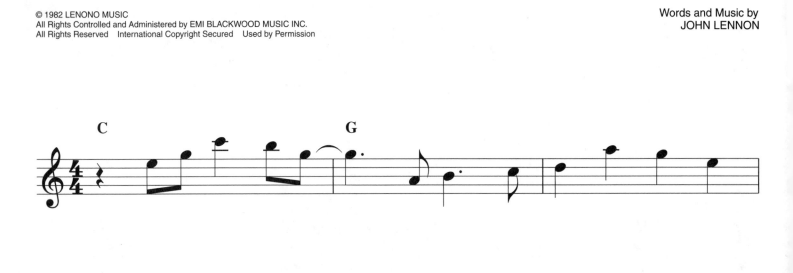

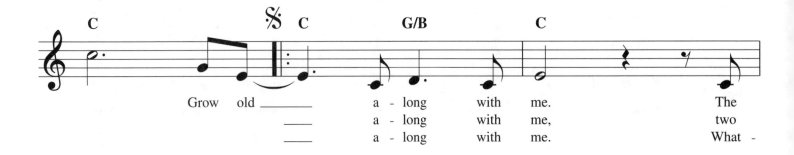

Grow old _____ a - long with me. The
_____ a - long with me, two
_____ a - long with me. What -

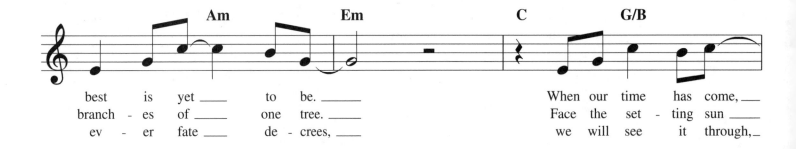

best is yet ___ to be. _____ When our time has come,
branch - es of ____ one tree. _____ Face the set - ting sun ___
ev - er fate ___ de - crees, ___ we will see it through, ___

_____ we will be as one. ___ God bless our
_____ when the day is done. ___
_____ for our love is true. ___

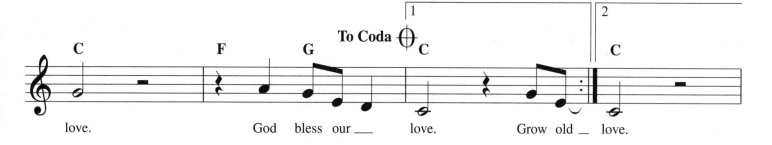

love.　　　　　　　God　bless　our ___　love.　　　Grow　old ___　love.

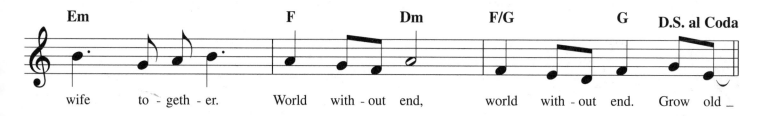

Spend - ing　our　lives _____　to - geth - er,　　　　man ___　and

wife　to - geth - er.　World　with - out　end,　　world　with - out　end.　Grow　old ___

love. God　bless　our ___　love.　　　　God　bless　our ___　love. _____

HELLO, YOUNG LOVERS
from THE KING AND I

Lyrics by OSCAR HAMMERSTEIN II
Music by RICHARD RODGERS

Hel -
lo young lov - ers, who - ev - er you are, I
brave, young lov - ers, and fol - low your star, be

hope your trou - bles are few. _____
brave and faith - ful and true. _____

All my good wish - es go with you to - night,
Cling ver - y close to each oth - er to - night,

I've been in love like you. _____ Be
I've been in love like

you. _____ I know how it feels to have

wings on your heels, and to fly down a

HERE, THERE AND EVERYWHERE

Words and Music by JOHN LENNON
and PAUL McCARTNEY

she's be-side me I know I need nev-er care. But to love her is to need her

ev-'ry-where, __ know-ing that love ___ is to share; ___

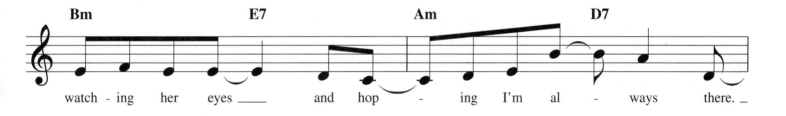

each one be-liev - ing that love ___ nev - er dies, ___

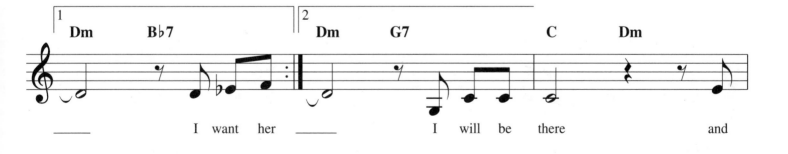

watch-ing her eyes ___ and hop - ing I'm al - ways there. _

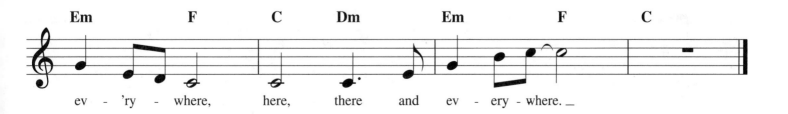

___ I want her ___ I will be there and

ev-'ry-where, here, there and ev-ery-where. _

HEY, GOOD LOOKIN'

Words and Music by
HANK WILLIAMS

Hey, hey, good look-in'
free and read-y so
what-cha got cook-in'? How's a-bout cook-in'
we can go stead-y. How's a-bout sav-in'
some-thin' up with me?
all your time for me?
Hey, sweet ba-by, don't you think may-be
No more look-in', I know I've been took-en
we could find us a brand new rec-i-pe?
How's a-bout keep-in' stead-y com-pa-ny?

HOW ARE THINGS IN GLOCCA MORRA

from FINIAN'S RAINBOW

Words by E.Y. HARBURG
Music by BURTON LANE

How are things in Gloc - ca Mor - ra? _____ Is that lit - tle brook still

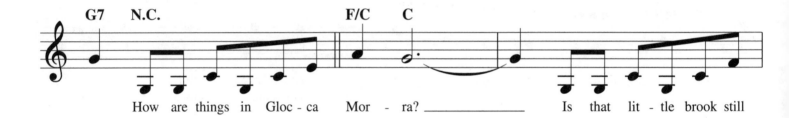

leap - ing there? _____ Does it still run down to Don - ny - cove _____ Through

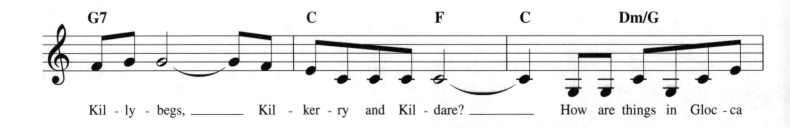

Kil - ly - begs, _____ Kil - ker - ry and Kil - dare? _____ How are things in Gloc - ca

HOW DEEP IS YOUR LOVE

from the Motion Picture SATURDAY NIGHT FEVER

Words and Music by BARRY GIBB,
MAURICE GIBB and ROBIN GIBB

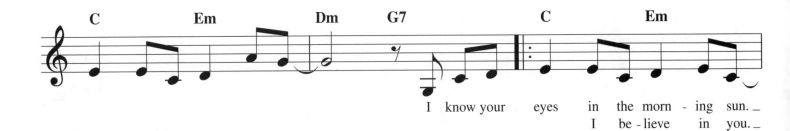

I know your eyes in the morn - ing sun.
I be - lieve in you.

____ I feel you touch ___ me in the pour - ing rain. ___ And the mo -
You know the door _____ to my ver - y soul _____ You're the light _

- ment that you wan - der far _____ from me, _____ I wan - na
_____ in my deep - est, dark - est hour: _____ you're my

feel you in my arms a - gain. ___ And you come ___ to me ___ on a sum -
sav - ior when I fall. ___ And you may ___ not think ___ I ___ care

Em ... Dm
- mer breeze; __ keep me warm _____ in your love, ___ then you soft -
_____ for you _____ when you know _____ down in - side ____ that I real -

B♭7 ... Em ... G7
- ly leave. __ And it's me you need __ to show; _____ how deep __
- ly do. ___ And it's me you need __ to show; _____ how deep __

C ... F
_____ is your love? __ How deep ___ is your _ love? I real - ly mean _ to learn. __

Fm ... C ... Gm _3_
_____ 'Cause we're liv - ing in a world of fools, ___ break - ing us

A7 ... Dm
down when they all _____ should let us be. _____ We be - long __

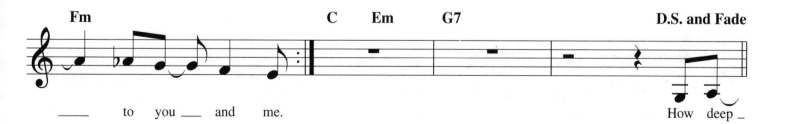

Fm ... C Em G7 D.S. and Fade
_____ to you __ and me. How deep __

I BELIEVE IN YOU AND ME
from the Touchstone Motion Picture THE PREACHER'S WIFE

Words and Music by DAVID WOLFERT
and SANDY LINZER

I be-lieve in you and me. I be-lieve that

we will be ____ in love e - ter - nal - ly. ____ Well, as far as I can see,

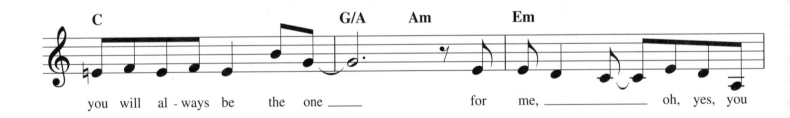

you will al - ways be the one ____ for me, ____ oh, yes, you

will. And I be-lieve in dreams a - gain. _ I be -lieve that love will nev - er end. And

like the riv - er finds _ the sea, I ____ was lost, ____ now I'm ____

free _____ 'cause I be-lieve in you and me. I will nev-er

leave your side. I will nev-er hurt your pride. __ When all the chips are down _ babe, then I will

al-ways be ____ a-round. _ Just to be right where you are, _____ my

love. _____ You know I love you, boy. I'll nev-er leave you out. __ I will al-ways

let you in, boy, oh, ba-by, to pla-ces no one's ev - er been. __ Deep _ in-side, _

_____ can't you see _____ that I be-lieve in you _____ and

IT COULD HAPPEN TO YOU
from the Paramount Picture AND THE ANGELS SING

Words by JOHNNY BURKE
Music by JAMES VAN HEUSEN

I CAN'T GET STARTED WITH YOU
from ZIEGFELD FOLLIES

Words by IRA GERSHWIN
Music by VERNON DUKE

I DIDN'T KNOW WHAT TIME IT WAS
from TOO MANY GIRLS

Words by LORENZ HART
Music by RICHARD RODGERS

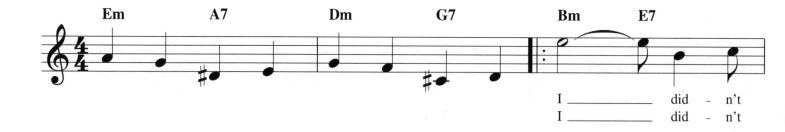

I _____ did - n't
I _____ did - n't

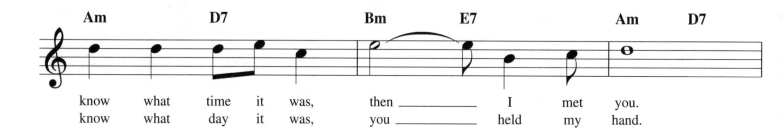

know   what   time   it   was,   then _____ I   met   you.
know   what   day   it   was,   you _____ held   my   hand.

Oh, _____ what   a   love - ly   time   it   was,   how   sub - lime   it   was,
Warm _____ like   the   month   of   May   it   was   and   I'll   say   it   was,

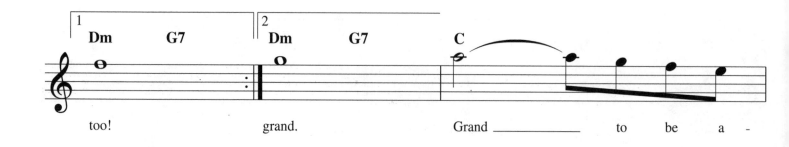

too!   grand.   Grand _____ to   be   a -

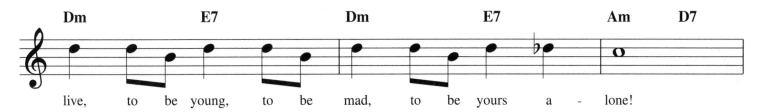

live, to be young, to be mad, to be yours a - lone!

Grand _____ to see your face, feel your touch, hear your voice say I'm all your

own! I _____ did - n't know what year it was,

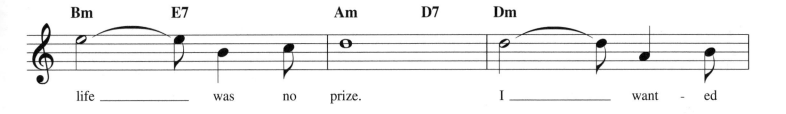

life _____ was no prize. I _____ want - ed

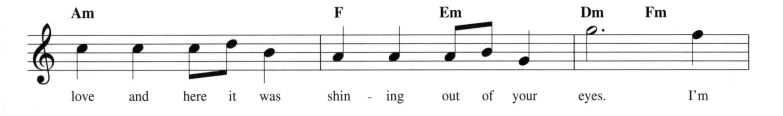

love and here it was shin - ing out of your eyes. I'm

wise _____ and I know what time it is now! _____

I LEFT MY HEART IN SAN FRANCISCO

Words by DOUGLASS CROSS
Music by GEORGE CORY

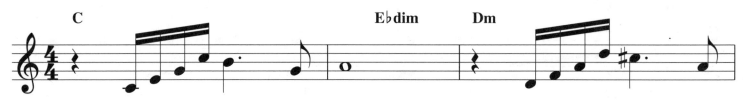

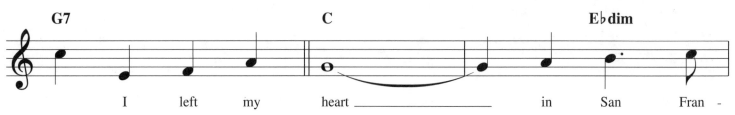

I left my heart _____ in San Fran -

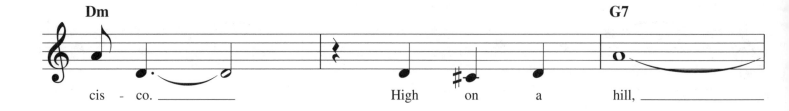

cis - co. _____ High on a hill, _____

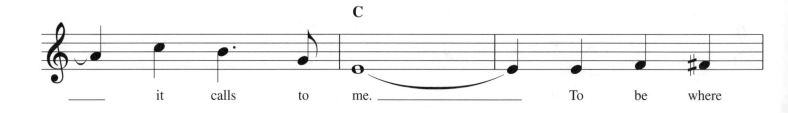

_____ it calls to me. _____ To be where

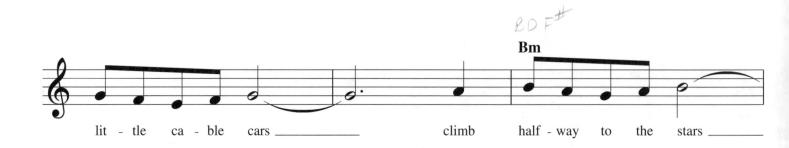

lit - tle ca - ble cars _____ climb half - way to the stars _____

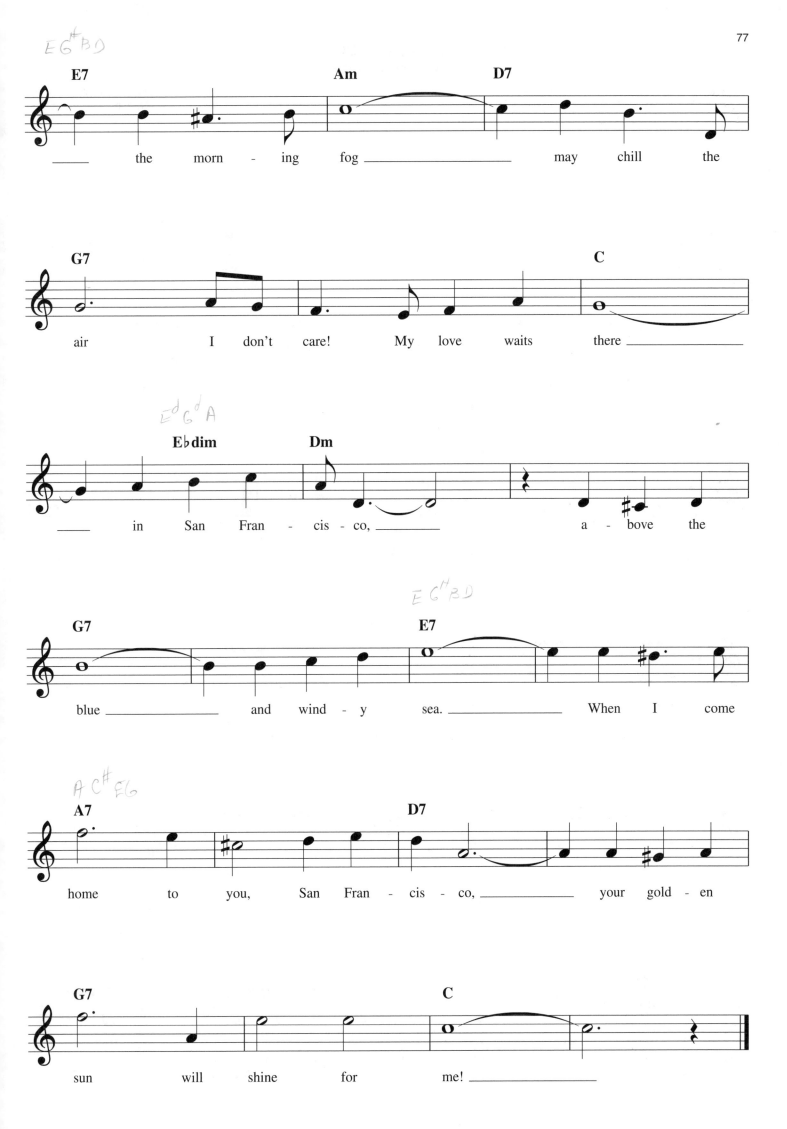

I WILL REMEMBER YOU
Theme from THE BROTHERS McMULLEN

Words and Music by SARAH McLACHLAN,
SEAMUS EGAN and DAVE MERENDA

I WISH I WERE IN LOVE AGAIN
from BABES IN ARMS

Words by LORENZ HART
Music by RICHARD RODGERS

81

wish I were in love a - gain! No _____ more
wish I were in love a - gain! No _____ more

pain, No _____ more strain,
care, No _____ de - spair.

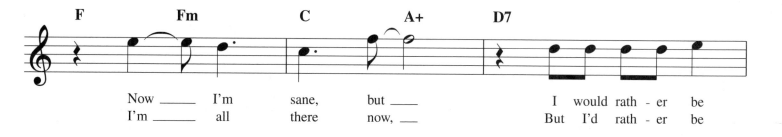

Now _____ I'm sane, but _____ I would rath - er be
I'm _____ all there now, _____ But I'd rath - er be

ga - ga! _____ The pulled out fur of cat and cur, the
punch - drunk! Be - lieve me sir, I much pre - fer the

fine mis - mat - ing of a him and her, I've learned my les - son but I
clas - sic bat - tle of a him and her, I don't like qui - et and I

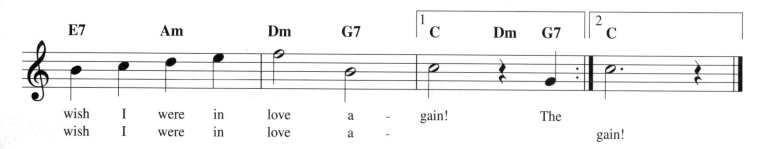

wish I were in love a - gain! The
wish I were in love a - gain!

I WRITE THE SONGS

Words and Music by
BRUCE JOHNSTON

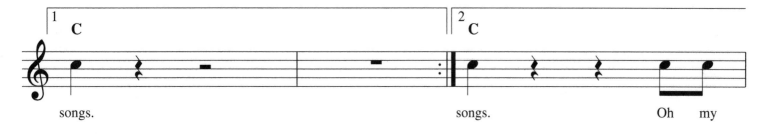

songs.   songs.   Oh my

mu - sic makes you dance and gives your spir - it to take a chance,

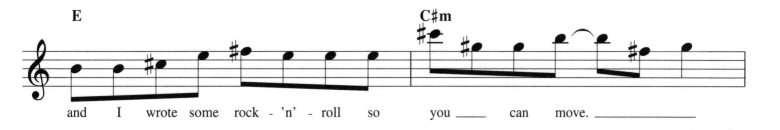

and I wrote some rock - 'n' - roll so you ____ can move. _____

Mu - sic fills your heart, well, that's a real fine place to start, it's from me,

D.S. al Coda

it's for you, it's from you, it's for me, it's a world ___ wide sym - pho - ny.

CODA

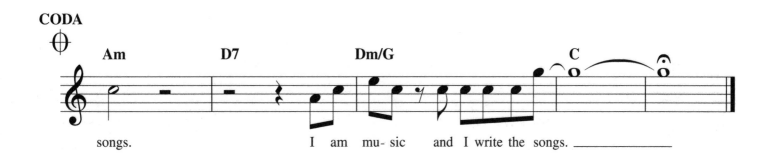

songs.   I am mu - sic and I write the songs. _____

I'LL BE SEEING YOU

from RIGHT THIS WAY

Lyric by IRVING KAHAL
Music by SAMMY FAIN

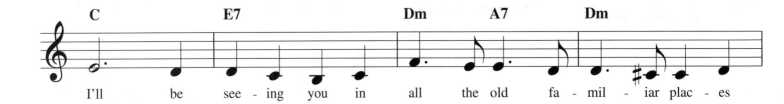

I'll be see - ing you in all the old fa - mil - iar plac - es

that this heart of mine em - brac - es all day thru. _____

In that small ca - fe, the park a - cross the way, the

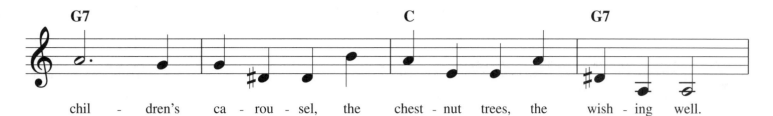

chil - dren's ca - rou - sel, the chest - nut trees, the wish - ing well.

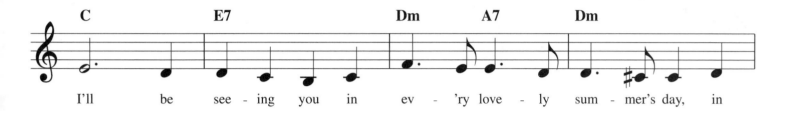

I'll be see - ing you in ev - 'ry love - ly sum - mer's day, in

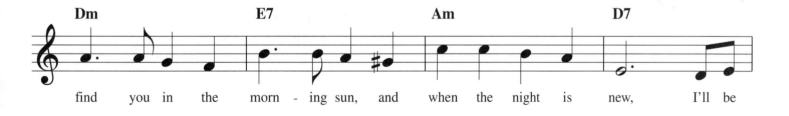

ev - 'ry-thing that's light and gay, I'll al - ways think of you that way I'll

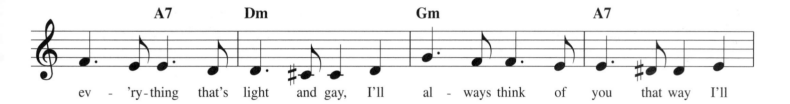

find you in the morn - ing sun, and when the night is new, I'll be

look - ing at the moon, _____ but I'll be see - ing you! _____

I'VE GOT THE WORLD ON A STRING

Lyric by TED KOEHLER
Music by HAROLD ARLEN

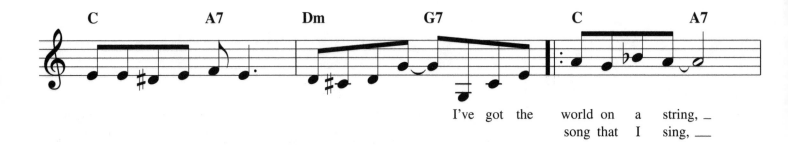

I've got the world on a string, _
song that I sing, __

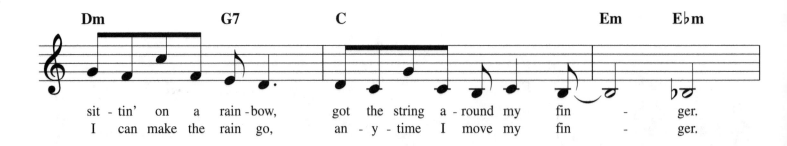

sit - tin' on a rain - bow, got the string a - round my fin - ger.
I can make the rain go, an - y - time I move my fin - ger.

What a world, what a _____ life, _ I'm in love! I've got a
Luck - y me, can't you ____ see, __ I'm in

love? _____ Life is a beau -ti - ful thing _____ as long as I hold the string, ___ I'd be a sil -ly so and so if I should ev -er let go. _____ I've got the world on a string, _ sit -tin' on a rain -bow, got the string a -round my fin -

- ger. What a world, what a _____ life, _ I'm in love. _____

IF

Words and Music by
DAVID GATES

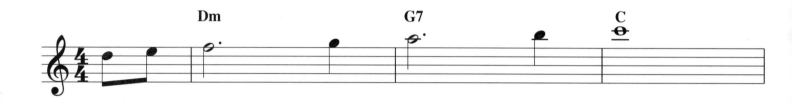

If a pic - ture paints a thou - sand words __ then why __
man could be two plac - es at ___ one time __

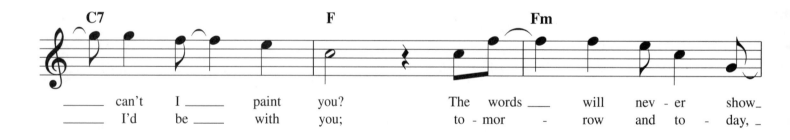

___ can't I ____ paint you?   The words ___ will nev - er show __
___ I'd be ___ with you;   to - mor - row and to - day, __

___ the you ___ I've come __ to know. ___   If a
___ be - side ___ you all ___ the way. ___   If the

face could launch a thou - sand ships, ___   then
world should stop re - volv - ing, spin - ning

where am I _____ to go? _____ There's no _____ one home _ but you. _
slow - ly down _ to die. _____ I'd spend _ the end _ with you. _

_____ You're all _____ that's left _ me to. And when _
_____ And when _____ the world _ was through then one _

_____ my love _____ for life _____ is run - ning _____
_____ by one _____ the stars _____ would all go _____

dry, you come and pour _____ your -
out. Then you and I _____ would

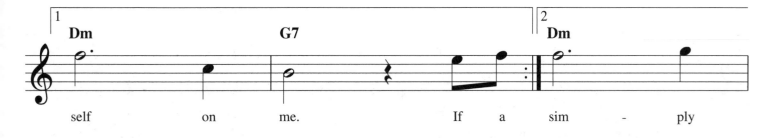

self on me. If a sim - ply

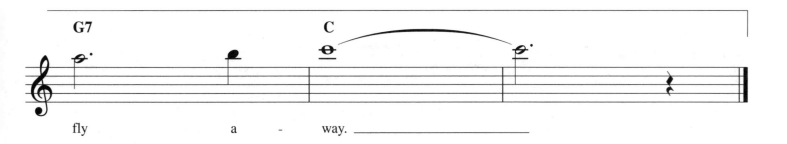

fly a - way. _____

IMAGINE

Words and Music by
JOHN LENNON

I - mag - ine there's   no   heav - en.

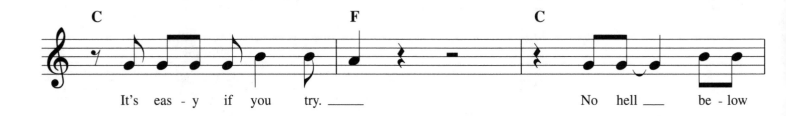

It's   eas - y   if   you   try. _____   No   hell ___   be - low

us,   a - bove   us   on - ly   sky.

I - mag - ine   all   the   peo - ple _____   liv - ing ___   for   to - day.

_____   Ah. _____   I - mag - ine there's   no   coun - tries.
                                                                              sions.

IN A SENTIMENTAL MOOD

Words and Music by DUKE ELLINGTON,
IRVING MILLS and MANNY KURTZ

In a sen-ti-men-tal

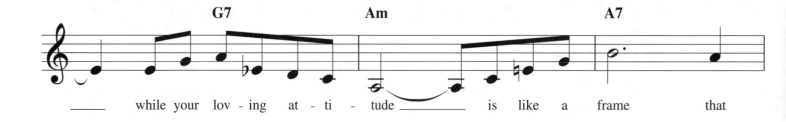

mood, _____ I can see the stars come through my room, _____

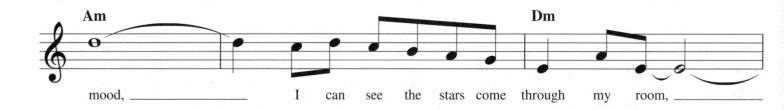

_____ while your lov-ing at-ti-tude _____ is like a frame that

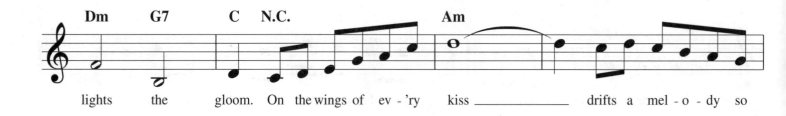

lights the gloom. On the wings of ev-'ry kiss _____ drifts a mel-o-dy so

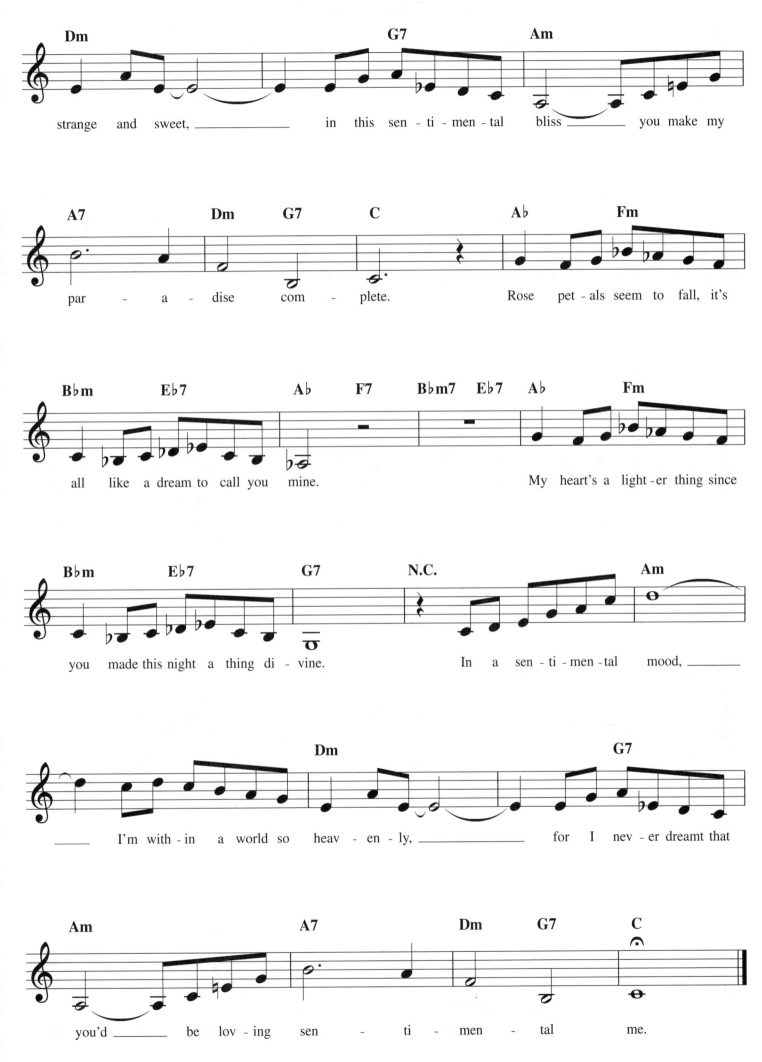

I'LL BE THERE

Words and Music by BERRY GORDY,
HAL DAVIS, WILLIE HUTCH and BOB WEST

You and I must make a pact. We must bring sal-

va - tion back. Where there is love _____ I'll _____ be there.

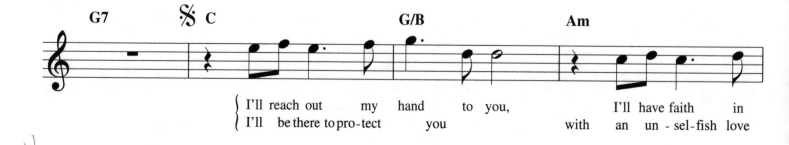

I'll reach out my hand to you, I'll have faith in
I'll be there to pro-tect you with an un-sel-fish love

CODA

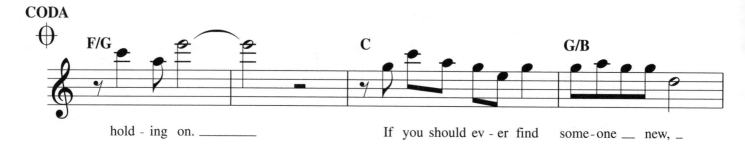

hold - ing on. _____ If you should ev - er find some-one __ new, __

I know she'd bet - ter be ____ good __ to you, _____ 'cause if she

does - n't then I'll be there. ____ Don't you know, ba - by

I'll be there, _____ I'll be there. _____

Just call my name _____ and I'll be there. _____

IN THE WEE SMALL HOURS OF THE MORNING

Words by BOB HILLIARD
Music by DAVID MANN

IT MIGHT AS WELL BE SPRING
from STATE FAIR

Lyrics by OSCAR HAMMERSTEIN II
Music by RICHARD RODGERS

IT NEVER ENTERED MY MIND
from HIGHER AND HIGHER

Words by LORENZ HART
Music by RICHARD RODGERS

F C G7 C G7 C Em

Once I laughed when

C Em C Em C Em

I heard you say - ing that I'd be play - ing sol - i - taire, __

C Em C Em F

un - eas - y in my eas - y chair. __ It nev - er en - tered my mind.

G7 C Em C Em

___ Once you told me I was mis - tak - en

C Em C Em C Em

that I'd a - wak - en with the sun __ and or - der or - ange

101

JAILHOUSE ROCK

Words and Music by JERRY LEIBER
and MIKE STOLLER

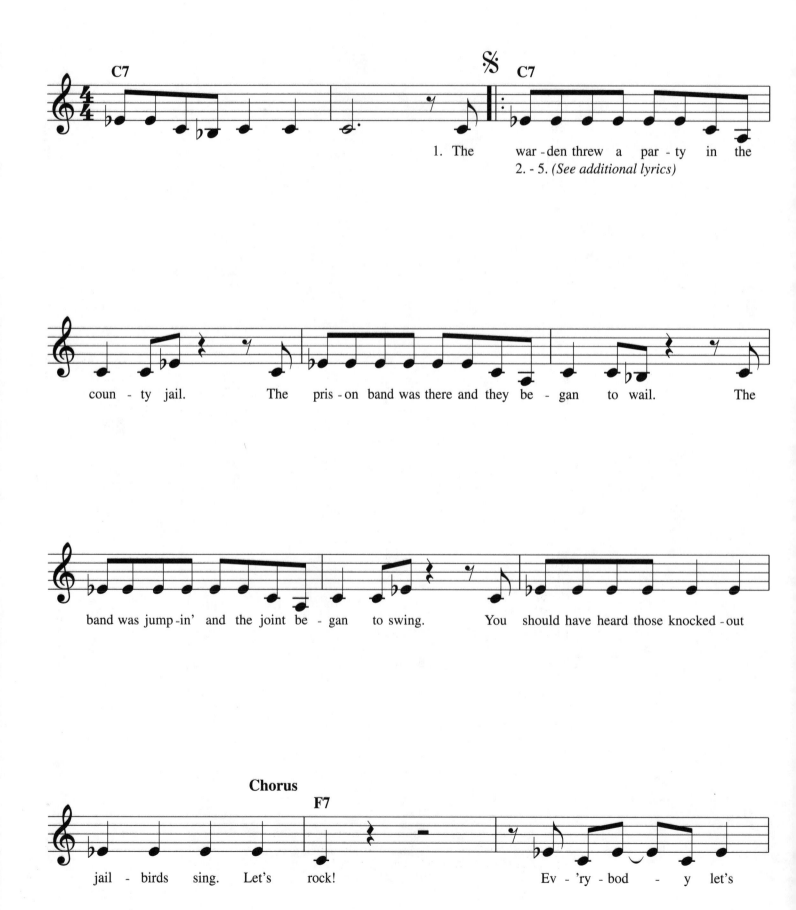

Additional Lyrics

2. Spider Murphy played the tenor saxophone
   Little Joe was blowin' on the slide trombone,
   The drummer boy from Illinois went crash, boom, bang;
   The whole rhythm section was the Purple Gang.
   (Chorus)

3. Number Forty-seven said to number Three;
   "You're the cutest jailbird I ever did see.
   I sure would be delighted with your company,
   Come on and do the Jailhouse Rock with me."
   (Chorus)

4. The sad sack was a-sittin' on a block of stone,
   Way over in the corner weeping all alone.
   The warden said: "Hey Buddy, don't you be so square,
   If you can't find a partner, use a wooden chair!"
   (Chorus)

5. Shifty Henry said to Bugs: "For heaven's sake,
   No one's lookin', now's our chance to make a break."
   Bugsy turned to Shifty and he said: "Nix, nix;
   I wanna stick around awhile and get my kicks."
   (Chorus)

KANSAS CITY

Words and Music by JERRY LEIBER
and MIKE STOLLER

THE LADY IS A TRAMP

Words by LORENZ HART
Music by RICHARD RODGERS

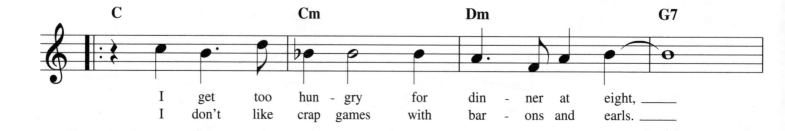

I get too hun - gry for din - ner at eight, ____
I don't like crap games with bar - ons and earls. ____

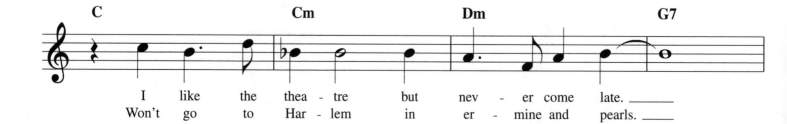

I like the thea - tre but nev - er come late. ____
Won't go to Har - lem in er - mine and pearls. ____

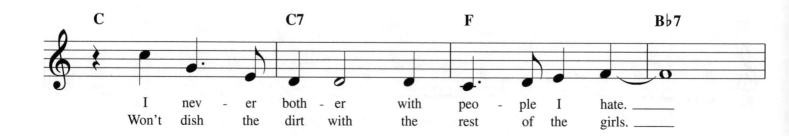

I nev - er both - er with peo - ple I hate. ____
Won't dish the dirt with the rest of the girls. ____

LOVE ME WITH ALL YOUR HEART
(Cuando calienta el sol)

Original Words and Music by CARLOS RIGUAL
and CARLOS A. MARTINOLI
English Words by SUNNY SKYLAR

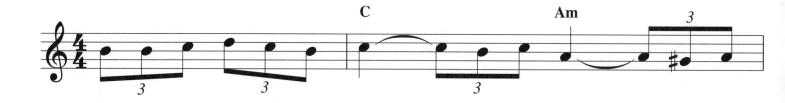

Love me with all your heart, __ that's all I

want, love. _____ Love me with all of your heart or not at all. _____

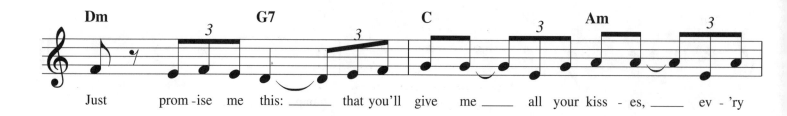

Just prom-ise me this: _____ that you'll give me _____ all your kiss-es, _____ ev-'ry

Spanish Lyrics

Cuando calienta el sol aqui en la playa
Siento tu cuerpo vibrar cerca de mí
Es tu palpitar es tu cara es tu pelo
Son tus besos me estremezco - o - o - o
Cuando calienta el sol aqui en la playa
Siento tu cuerpo vibrar cerca de mí
Es tu palpitar tu recuerdo mi locura
Mi delirio me estremezco - o - o - o
Cuando calienta el sol.

LAZY RIVER

from THE BEST YEARS OF OUR LIVES

Words and Music by HOAGY CARMICHAEL
and SIDNEY ARODIN

Up a la-zy riv-er by the old mill-run, that la-zy, la-zy riv-er in the noon-day sun, lin-ger in the shade of a kind old tree; throw a-way your trou-bles, dream a dream with me. __ Up a la-zy riv-er where the rob-in's song a-wakes a bright new morn-ing, we can loaf a-long. Blue skies up a-bove, ev-'ry-one's in love, up a la-zy riv-er, how hap-py you can be, up a la-zy riv-er with me.

MISTY

Words by JOHNNY BURKE
Music by ERROLL GARNER

MAKIN' WHOOPEE!

Lyrics by GUS KAHN
Music by WALTER DONALDSON

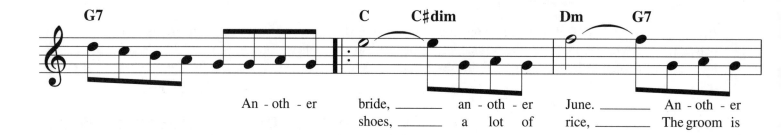

An - oth - er bride, _____ an - oth - er June. _____ An - oth - er
shoes, _____ a lot of rice, _____ The groom is

sun - ny hon - ey - moon; _____ An - oth - er sea - son, _____ an - oth - er
ner - vous, _____ he an - swers twice; _____ It's real - ly kill - ing, _____ that he's so

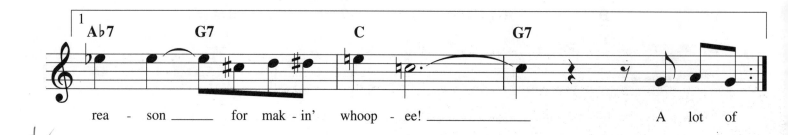

rea - son _____ for mak - in' whoop - ee! _____   A lot of

MEMORIES OF YOU

Lyric by ANDY RAZAF
Music by EUBIE BLAKE

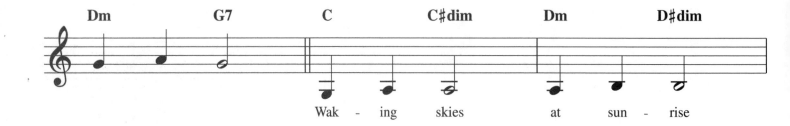

Wak - ing   skies   at   sun - rise

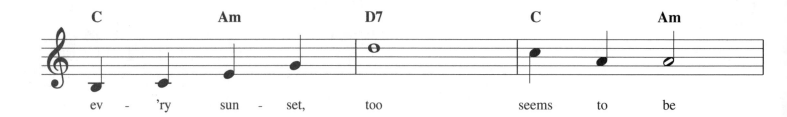

ev - 'ry   sun - set,   too   seems   to   be

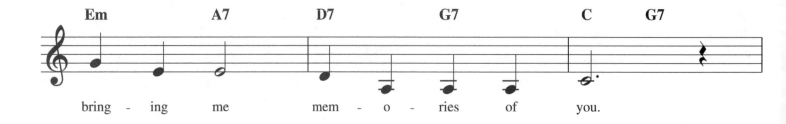

bring - ing   me   mem - o - ries   of   you.

Here   and   there,   ev - 'ry - where   scenes   that   we   once

MEMORY
from CATS

Music by ANDREW LLOYD WEBBER
Text by TREVOR NUNN after T.S. ELIOT

117

MICHELLE

Words and Music by JOHN LENNON
and PAUL McCARTNEY

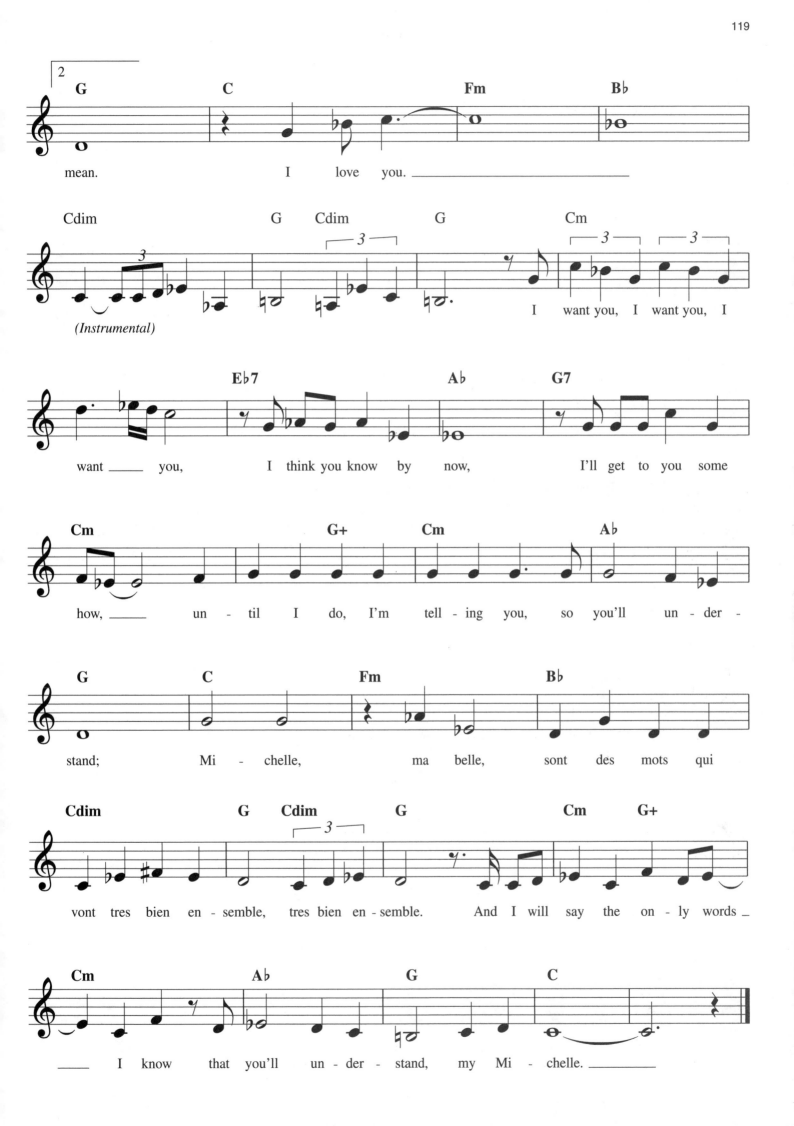

MONA LISA
from the Paramount Picture CAPTAIN CAREY, U.S.A.

Words and Music by JAY LIVINGSTON
and RAY EVANS

Mo - na

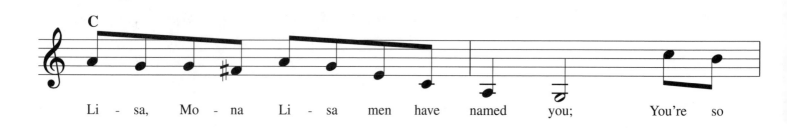

Li - sa, Mo - na Li - sa men have named you; You're so

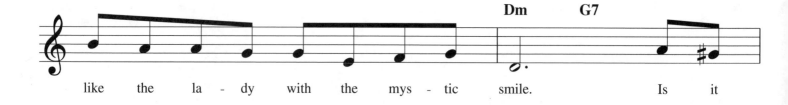

like the la - dy with the mys - tic smile. Is it

on - ly 'cause you're lone - ly _____ they have blamed you for that

Mo - na Li - sa strange - ness _____ in your smile? Do you smile to tempt a lov - er, _____ Mo - na Li - sa, _____ or is this your way to hide a bro - ken heart? Man - y dreams have been brought to your door - step. They just lie there, and they die there. Are you warm, are you real, Mo - na

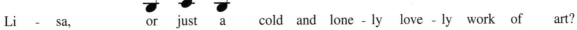

Li - sa, or just a cold and lone - ly love - ly work of art?

MOON RIVER
from the Paramount Picture BREAKFAST AT TIFFANY'S

Words by JOHNNY MERCER
Music by HENRY MANCINI

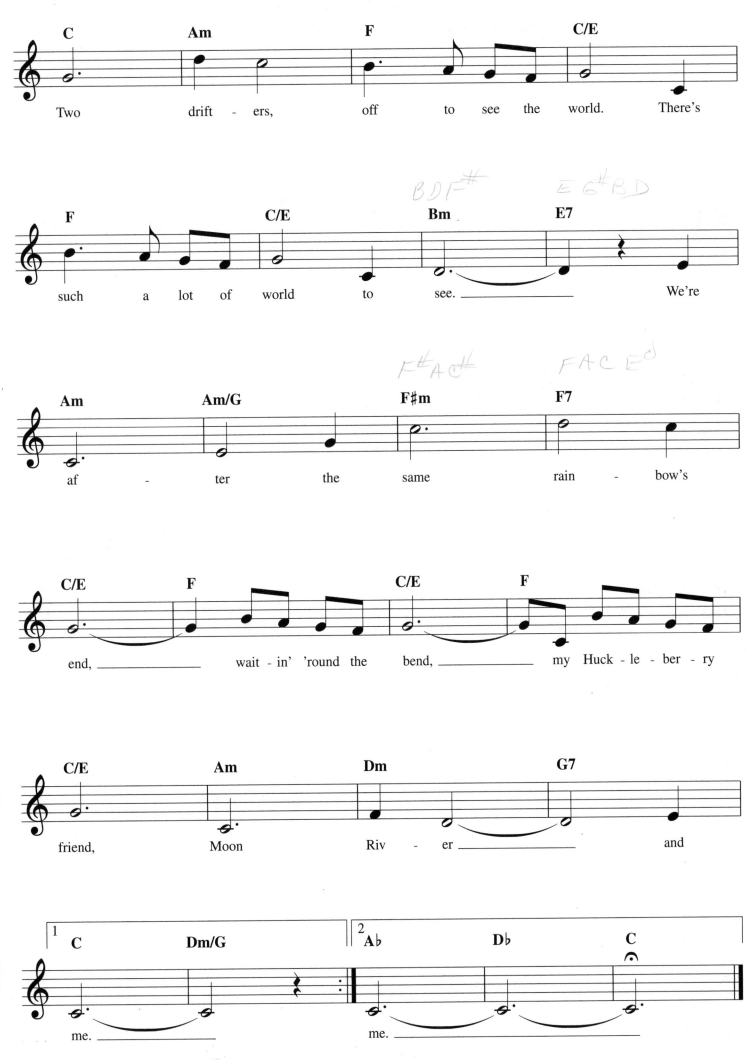

MOONLIGHT IN VERMONT

Words and Music by JOHN BLACKBURN
and KARL SUESSDORF

Pen - nies in a stream,

fall - ing leaves a sy - ca - more, moon - light in Ver -

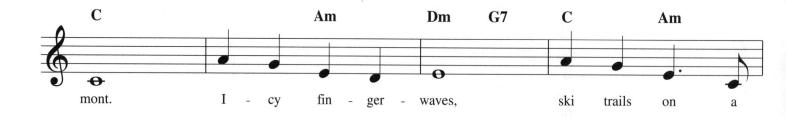

mont. I - cy fin - ger - waves, ski trails on a

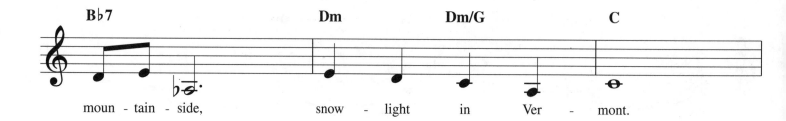

moun - tain - side, snow - light in Ver - mont.

MY HEART WILL GO ON
(Love Theme from 'Titanic')
from the Paramount and Twentieth Century Fox Motion Picture TITANIC

Music by JAMES HORNER
Lyric by WILL JENNINGS

Once more you o-pen the door ____ and you're

here in my heart, and my heart will go on and

on. *(Instrumental)*

on. *(Instrumental)*

You're here, there's noth-ing I fear ____ and I know ____

____ that my heart will go on. ____

We'll stay for-ev-er this way. ____ You are

safe in my heart, and my heart will go on and on.

MY GIRL

Words and Music by WILLIAM "SMOKEY" ROBINSON
and RONALD WHITE

I guess you say, what can make me feel this way?

My girl, _____ talk-ing 'bout my ___ girl. _____

I've got sun-shine on a cloud - y day ___ with my girl; _____ I've

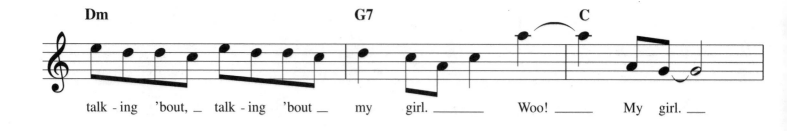

e - ven got the month of May with my girl. _____ Talk -ing 'bout, ___

talk - ing 'bout, _ talk -ing 'bout _ my girl. _____ Woo! _____ My girl. ___

That's all _____ I can talk a - bout, is my girl.

(YOU MAKE ME FEEL LIKE) A NATURAL WOMAN

Words and Music by GERRY GOFFIN,
CAROLE KING and JERRY WEXLER

THE NEARNESS OF YOU

from the Paramount Picture ROMANCE IN THE DARK

Words by NED WASHINGTON
Music by HOAGY CARMICHAEL

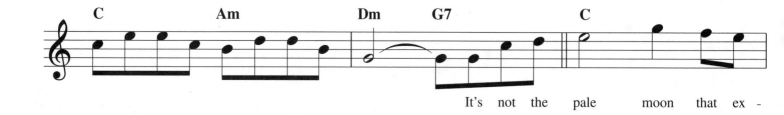

It's not the pale moon that ex -

cites me, that thrills and de - lights me. Oh, no _____

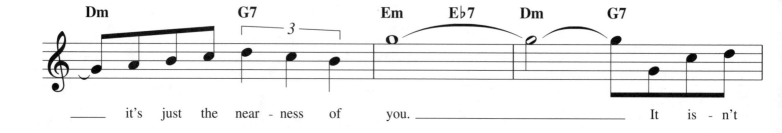

_____ it's just the near - ness of you. _____ It is - n't

your sweet con - ver - sa - tion that brings this sen - sa - tion. Oh,

A NIGHTINGALE SANG IN BERKELEY SQUARE

Lyric by ERIC MASCHWITZ
Music by MANNING SHERWIN

That

cer - tain night, the night we met, there was mag - ic a - broad in the air. There were
strange it was, how sweet and strange, there was nev - er a dream to com - pare. With that

an - gels din - ing at the Ritz, and a { night - in - gale sang in Berk - 'ley
ha - zy, cra - zy night we met, when a {

Square.
{ I may be right, I may be wrong, but I'm
This heart of mine beats loud and fast like a

per - fect - ly will - ing to swear that when you turned and smiled at me, a
mer - ry - go - round in a fair. For we were danc - ing cheek to cheek and a {

night - in - gale sang in Berk - 'ley Square.
{ The moon that lin - gered o - ver
When down came steal - ing up all

ONE LESS BELL TO ANSWER

Lyric by HAL DAVID
Music by BURT BACHARACH

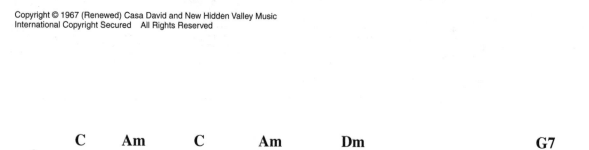

One less

bell to an - swer. One less egg to fry. One less man to pick up af - ter.

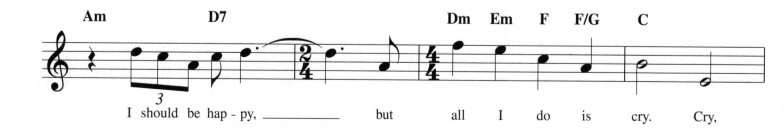

I should be hap - py, _____ but all I do is cry. Cry,

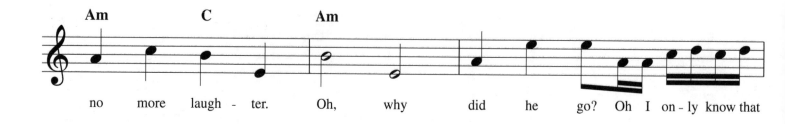

no more laugh - ter. Oh, why did he go? Oh I on - ly know that

since he left my life's so emp - ty. Though I try to for - get, it just

PEOPLE
from FUNNY GIRL

Words by BOB MERRILL
Music by JULE STYNE

RELEASE ME

Words and Music by ROBERT YOUNT,
EDDIE MILLER and DUB WILLIAMS

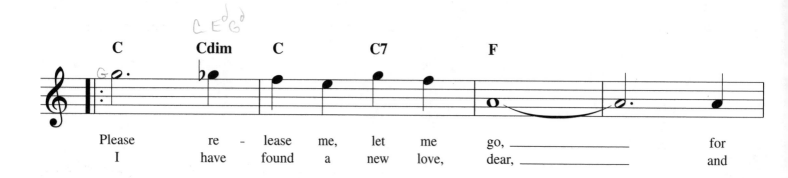

Please re - lease me, let me go, _____ for
I have found a new love, dear, _____ and

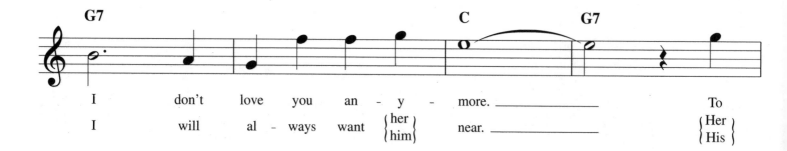

I don't love you an - y - more. _____ To
I will al - ways want {her}{him} near. _____ {Her}{His}

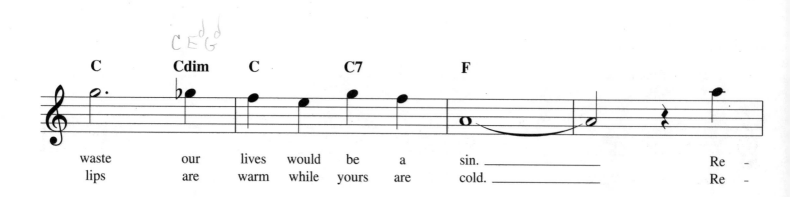

waste our lives would be a sin. _____ Re -
lips are warm while yours are cold. _____ Re -

ROCKIN' CHAIR

Words and Music by
HOAGY CARMICHAEL

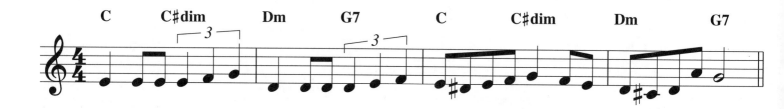

Old rock -in' chair's got me, _____ cane by my side.

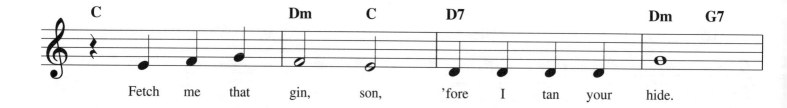

Fetch me that gin, son, 'fore I tan your hide.

Can't get from this cab - in, _____ goin' no - where.

SKYLARK

Words by JOHNNY MERCER
Music by HOAGY CARMICHAEL

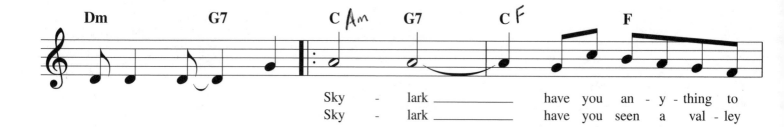

Sky - lark _____ have you an - y - thing to
Sky - lark _____ have you seen a val - ley

say   to   me? _____ Won't you tell me where my   love can   be? _____
green with   spring? _____ Where my heart can go a   jour - ney - ing? _____

_____ Is there a mead - ow in the   mist, _____ where some - one's wait - ing to be kissed?
_____ O - ver the shad - ows and the

SOLITUDE

Words and Music by DUKE ELLINGTON,
EDDIE DE LANGE and IRVING MILLS

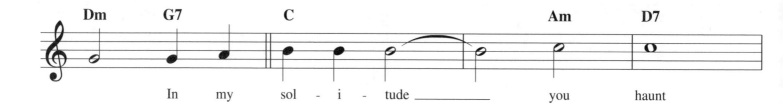

In my sol - i - tude _____ you haunt

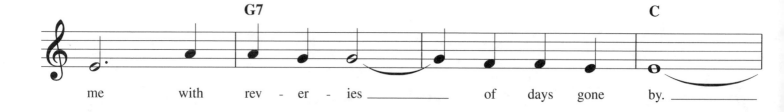

me with rev - er - ies _____ of days gone by. _____

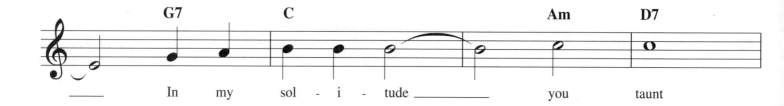

_____ In my sol - i - tude _____ you taunt

me with mem - o - ries _____ that nev - er die. _____

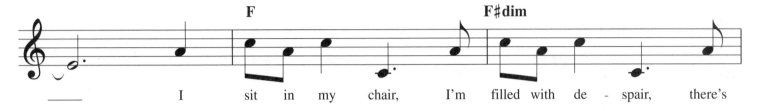

_____ I sit in my chair, I'm filled with de - spair, there's

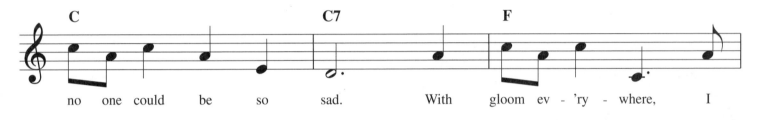

no one could be so sad. With gloom ev - 'ry - where, I

sit and I stare. I know that I'll soon go mad. In my

sol - i - tude _____ I'm pray - ing dear

Lord a - bove _____ send back my love. _____

SOME ENCHANTED EVENING
from SOUTH PACIFIC

Lyrics by OSCAR HAMMERSTEIN II
Music by RICHARD RODGERS

SOMEBODY LOVES ME

Words by B.G. DeSYLVA and BALLARD MacDONALD
Music by GEORGE GERSHWIN
French Version by EMELIA RENAUD

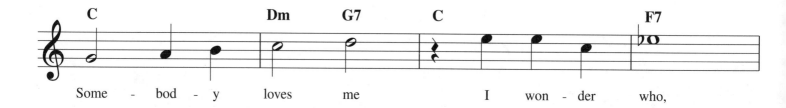

Some - bod - y loves me   I won - der who,

I won - der who { she / he } can be; _____

Some - bod - y loves me   I wish I knew,

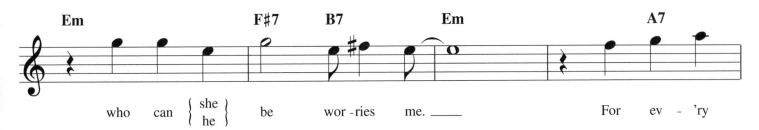

who can { she / he } be wor-ries me. _____ For ev - 'ry

{ girl / boy } who pass - es me I shout, Hey! may - be

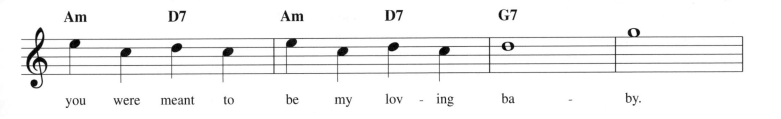

you were meant to be my lov - ing ba - by.

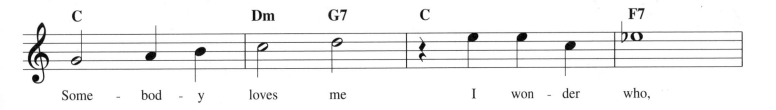

Some - bod - y loves me I won - der who,

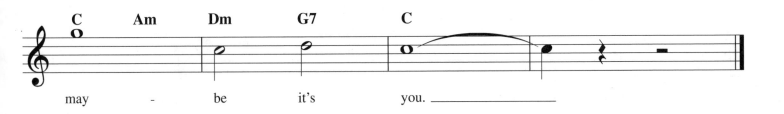

may - be it's you. _____

SOMETHING

Words and Music by
GEORGE HARRISON

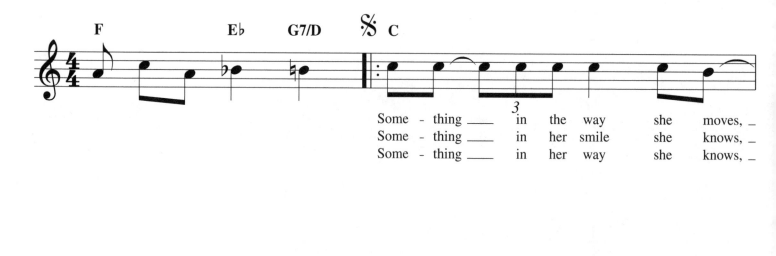

Some - thing ____ in the way she moves, _
Some - thing ____ in her smile she knows, _
Some - thing ____ in her way she knows, _

____ at - tracts me like no oth - er lov - er.
____ that I don't need no oth - er lov - er.
____ and all I have to do is think of her.

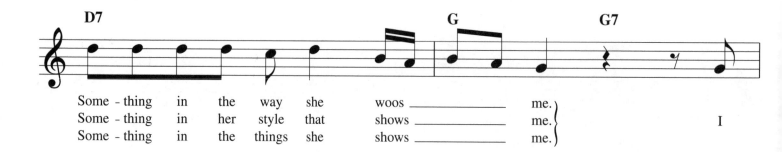

Some - thing in the way she woos ____ me.
Some - thing in her style that shows ____ me.
Some - thing in the things she shows ____ me.

I

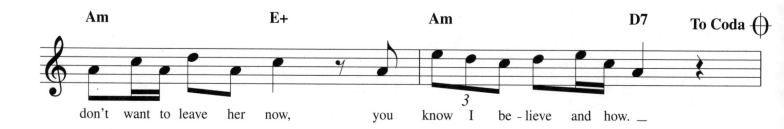

don't want to leave her now,   you know I be - lieve and how. _

(Instrumental)

(Instrumental)

You're ask - ing me will my love grow, I don't

know, ____ I ____ don't know.

You stick a - round now, it may

show, I don't know, ____ I ____ don't know.

D.S. al Coda

CODA

(Instrumental)

SOMETIMES WHEN WE TOUCH

Words by DAN HILL
Music by BARRY MANN

sides. *(Instrumental)*

Ro - sides. At

times I'd like __ to break __ you and drive _____ you to _____ your knees. __

_____ At times I'd like __ to break __ through _____ and

D.S. al Coda

hold __ you end - less - ly. _____ At

CODA

sides. *(Instrumental)*

rit.

SAVE THE BEST FOR LAST

Words and Music by PHIL GALDSTON,
JON LIND and WENDY WALDMAN

Some-times the snow __

_____ comes down _ in June. ___   Some-times the sun ____ goes 'round __ the moon. __
_____ you came _ to me _____ when some sil - ly girl ____ had set _____ you free. __
_____ comes down _ in June. ___   Some-times the sun ____ goes 'round __ the moon. _

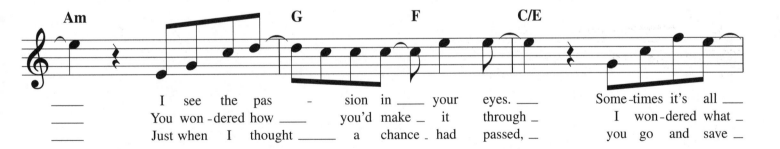

_____ I see the pas - sion in ____ your eyes. ___   Some-times it's all ___
_____ You won-dered how ____ you'd make _ it through _   I won-dered what _
_____ Just when I thought _____ a chance _ had passed, _   you go and save _

To Coda ⊕

_____ a big ___ sur - prise. ___   'Cause there was a time ____ when all ___ I did ___
_____ was wrong _ with you. ____   'Cause how could you give ____ your love _ to some -
_____ the best __ for last. __

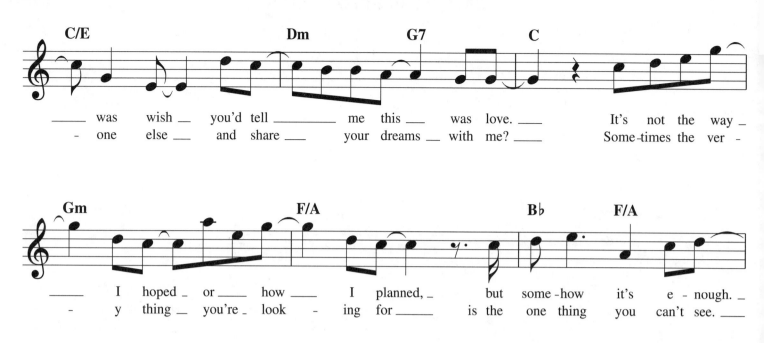

_____ was wish _____ you'd tell _____ me this ___ was love. _____ It's not the way _
- one else ___ and share ____ your dreams ___ with me? _____ Some-times the ver -

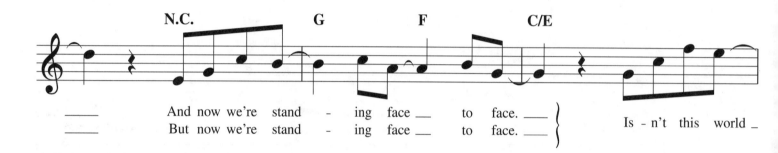

_____ I hoped _ or _____ how _____ I planned, _ but some-how it's e - nough. _
- y thing _ you're _ look - ing for _____ is the one thing you can't see. _

_____ And now we're stand - ing face _ to face. _____
_____ But now we're stand - ing face _ to face. _____
_____ Is - n't this world _

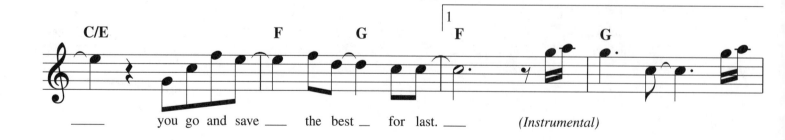

_____ a cra - zy place? _ Just when I thought _____ our chance _ had passed, _

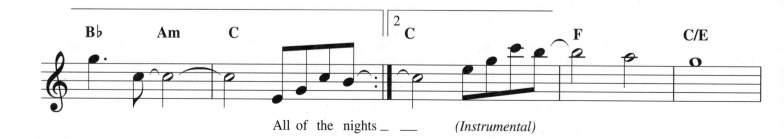

_____ you go and save ___ the best _ for last. _____ *(Instrumental)*

All of the nights _ ___ *(Instrumental)*

SOPHISTICATED LADY

Words and Music by DUKE ELLINGTON,
IRVING MILLS and MITCHELL PARISH

They say _____ in - to your ear - ly life ro - mance came, _____ and in this heart of yours burned a flame, _____ a flame that flick-ered one day and died a - way. Then, _____ with dis - il - lu - sion deep in your eyes, _____ you learned that

fools in love soon grow wise. _____ The years have changed you, some-how;   I

STAND BY ME

Words and Music by BEN E. KING,
JERRY LEIBER and MIKE STOLLER

stand _____ by me, oh, stand, _____ stand by me,

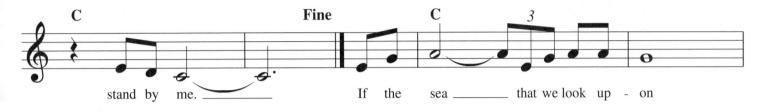

stand by me. _____ If the sea _____ that we look up - on

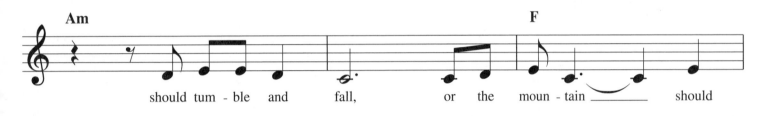

should tum - ble and fall, or the moun - tain _____ should

crum - ble _____ in the sea, I won't cry, I won't

cry, no _____ I _____ won't shed a tear just as

long _____ as you stand, _____ stand by me. So, dar - ling, dar - ling,

STAR DUST

Words by MITCHELL PARISH
Music by HOAGY CARMICHAEL

...And now the pur-ple dusk of twi-light time steals a-cross the mead-ows of my heart. High up in the sky the lit-tle stars climb, al-ways re-mind-ing me that we're a-part. You wan-dered down the lane and far a-way, leav-ing me a song that will not die. Love is now the star dust of yes-ter-day, the mu-sic of the years gone

STELLA BY STARLIGHT

from the Paramount Picture THE UNINVITED

Words by NED WASHINGTON
Music by VICTOR YOUNG

The song _____ a rob-in sings _____ through

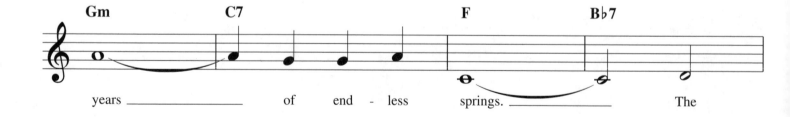

years _____ of end-less springs. _____ The

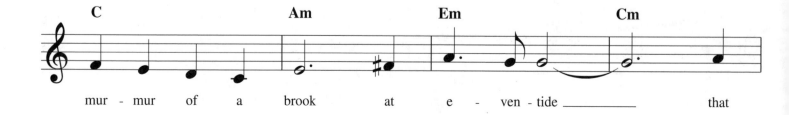

mur-mur of a brook at e-ven-tide _____ that

TANGERINE

from the Paramount Picture THE FLEET'S IN

Words by JOHNNY MERCER
Music by VICTOR SCHERTZINGER

Tan - ger -

ine, _____ she is all they claim _____ with her

eyes of night and lips as bright as flame. _____ Tan - ger -

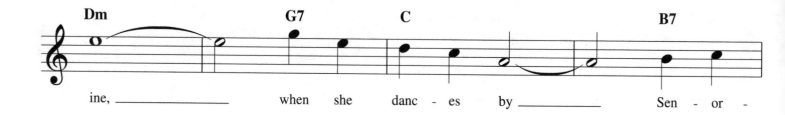

ine, _____ when she danc - es by _____ Sen - or -

i - tas stare and ca - bal - le - ros sigh. _____ And I've

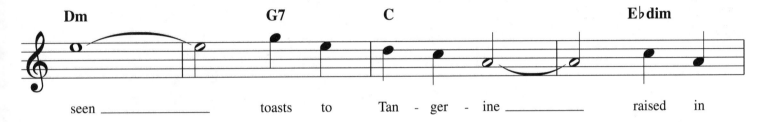

seen _____ toasts to Tan - ger - ine _____ raised in

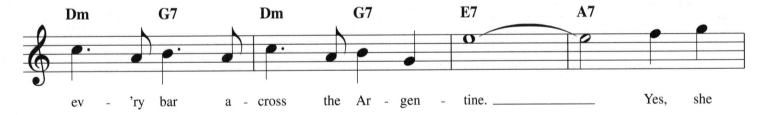

ev - 'ry bar a - cross the Ar - gen - tine. _____ Yes, she

has them all on the run but her heart be - longs to just one. Her

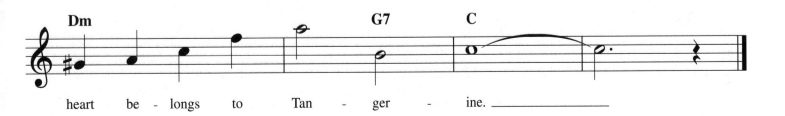

heart be - longs to Tan - ger - ine. _____

TEARS IN HEAVEN

Words and Music by ERIC CLAPTON
and WILL JENNINGS

Would you know   my   name _____   if   I   saw you in heav-
Would you know   my   hand _____   if   I   saw you in heav-
Would you know   my   name _____   if   I   saw you in heav-

en?   Would it   be   the same _____   if   I   saw you in heav-
en?   Would you help me stand _____   if   I   saw you in heav-
en?   Would you be   the same _____   if   I   saw you in heav-

en?   (1., 3.) I   must   be strong __   and car - ry on __
en?   (2.) I'll find   my   way ___   through night and day __
en?

174

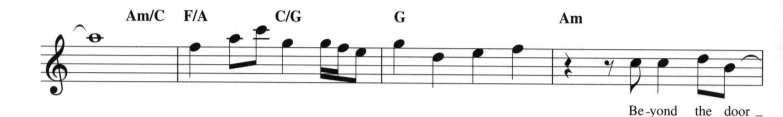

Be-yond the door _

there's peace, I'm sure, _____ and I know _

_____ there'll be no more _ tears in heav - en. *(Instrumental)*

D.S. al Coda

CODA

en. *(Instrumental)*

THIS CAN'T BE LOVE
from THE BOYS FROM SYRACUSE

Words by LORENZ HART
Music by RICHARD RODGERS

TENNESSEE WALTZ

Words and Music by REDD STEWART
and PEE WEE KING

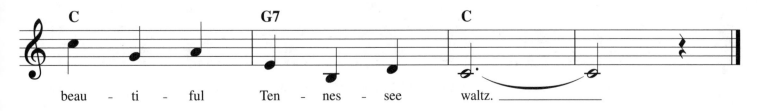

THERE'S A SMALL HOTEL

from ON YOUR TOES

Words by LORENZ HART
Music by RICHARD RODGERS

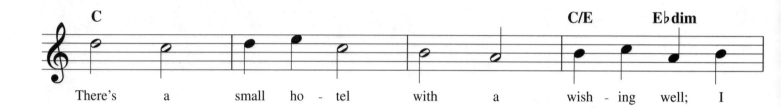

There's a small ho - tel with a wish - ing well; I

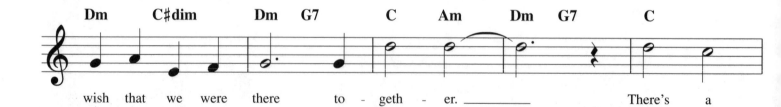

wish that we were there to - geth - er. _____ There's a

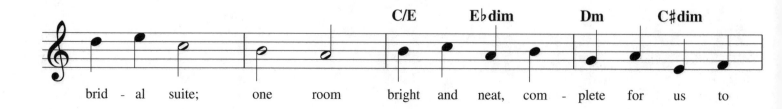

brid - al suite; one room bright and neat, com - plete for us to

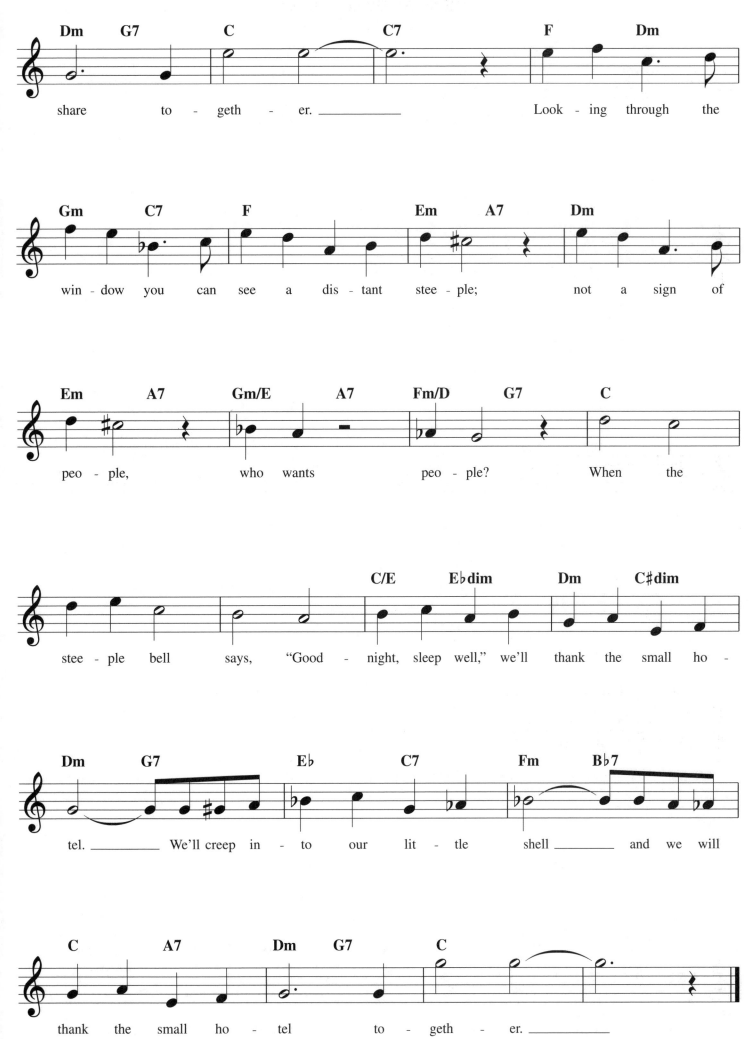

UNCHAINED MELODY

Lyrics by HY ZARET
Music by ALEX NORTH

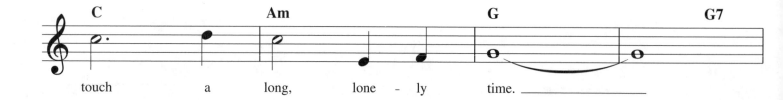

Oh, my love, my dar - ling, I've hun - gered for your

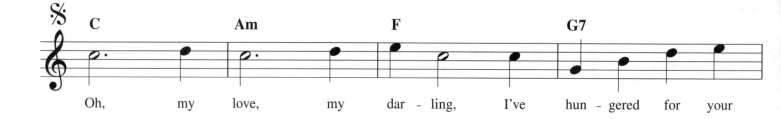

touch a long, lone - ly time. _____

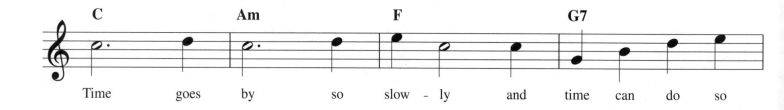

Time goes by so slow - ly and time can do so

much,　　are　you　　still　　mine? _____ I

need　your　love, _____ I　need　your　love, _____ God

speed　your　love _____ to　　me! _____

Lone - ly　riv - ers　　flow _____ to　the　sea, _____ to　the
Love - ly　riv - ers　　sigh, _____ "Wait　for　me, _____ wait　for

sea.　　　To　the　o - pen　arms _____ of　the
me!"　　I'll　be　com - ing　home, _____ wait　for

sea. _____

me. _____

VALENTINE

Words and Music by JACK KUGELL
and JIM BRICKMAN

THE VERY THOUGHT OF YOU

Words and Music by
RAY NOBLE

The ver - y

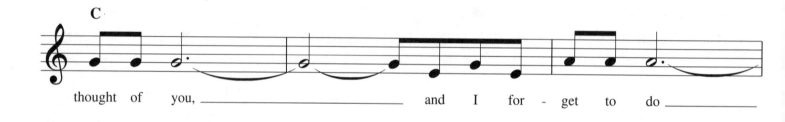

thought of you, _____ and I for - get to do _____

_____ the lit - tle or - di - nar - y things that ev - 'ry - one

ought to do. _____ I'm liv - ing in a kind of day - dream, I'm

hap - py as a king, and fool - ish tho' it may seem, to

WALKIN' AFTER MIDNIGHT

Lyrics by DON HECHT
Music by ALAN W. BLOCK

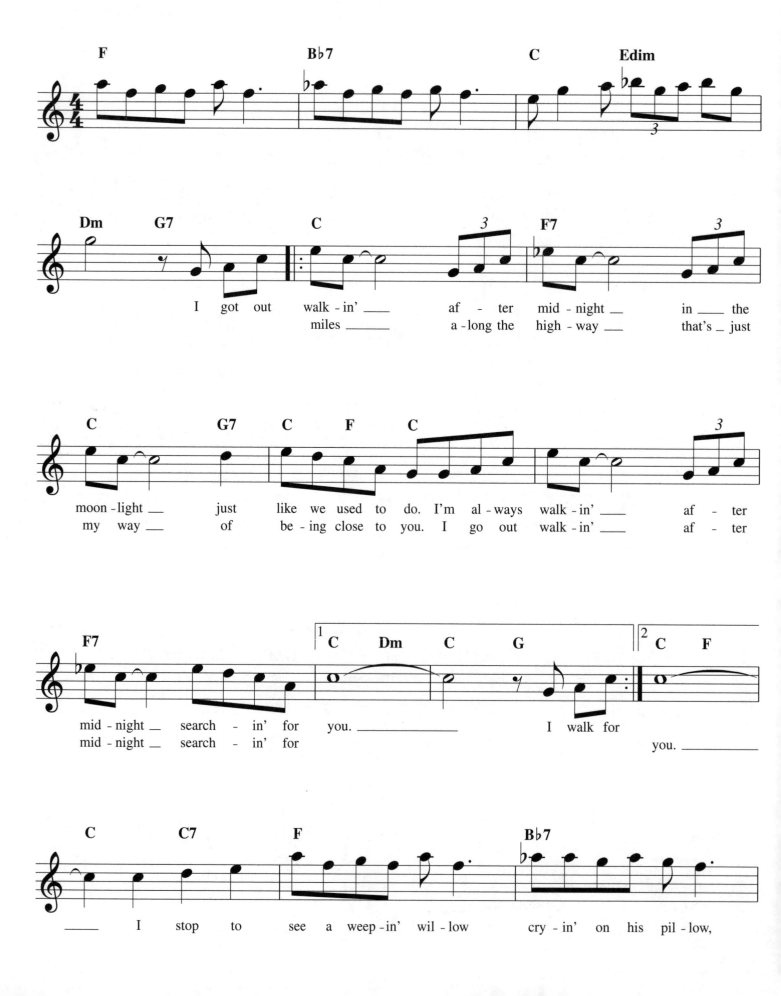

THE WAY WE WERE

Words by ALAN and MARILYN BERGMAN
Music by MARVIN HAMLISCH

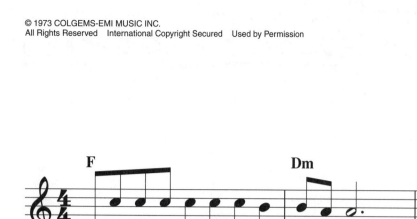

Mem - 'ries _____ light the cor - ners of my mind.
pic - tures _____ of the smiles we left be - hind,

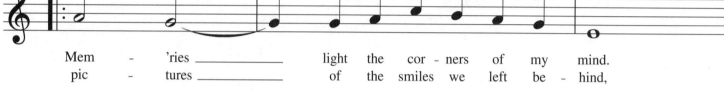

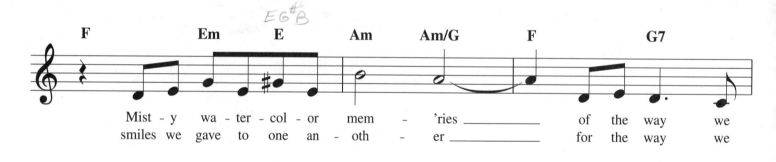

Mist - y wa - ter - col - or mem - 'ries _____ of the way we
smiles we gave to one an - oth - er _____ for the way we

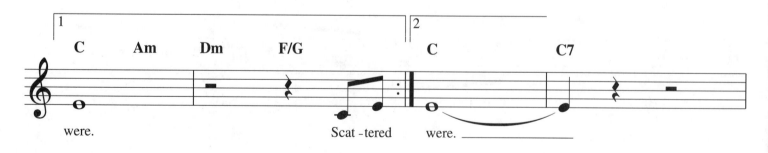

were.   Scat - tered   were. _____

Can it be that it was all so sim - ple then,   or has time re - writ - ten ev - 'ry

WHAT A WONDERFUL WORLD

Words and Music by GEORGE DAVID WEISS
and BOB THIELE

WHAT'LL I DO?
from MUSIC BOX REVUE OF 1924

Words and Music by
IRVING BERLIN

WITH A SONG IN MY HEART

from SPRING IS HERE

Words by LORENZ HART
Music by RICHARD RODGERS

WHAT'S NEW?

Words by JOHNNY BURKE
Music by BOB HAGGART

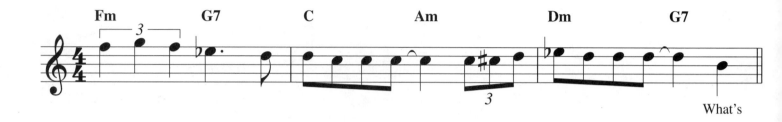

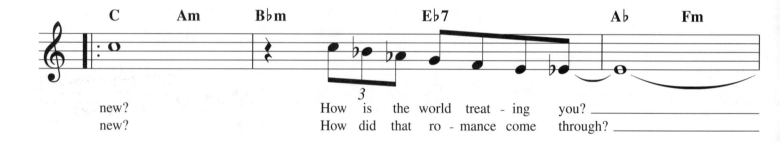

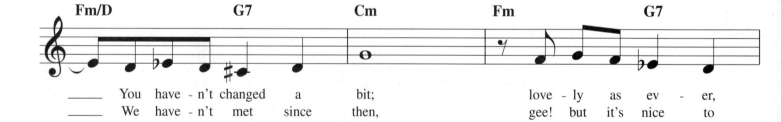

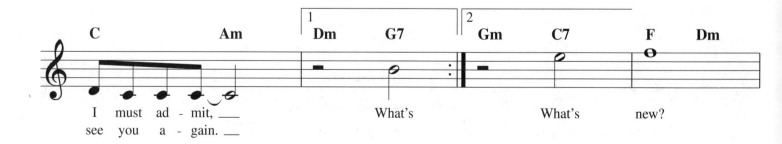

WHERE THE BOYS ARE

Words and Music by HOWARD GREENFIELD
and NEIL SEDAKA

Where _____ the

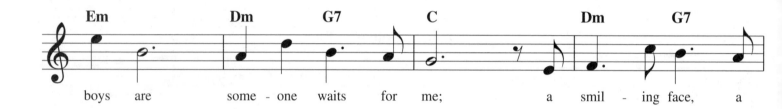

boys are some - one waits for me; a smil - ing face, a

warm em-brace, two arms to hold me ten-der - ly. Where _____ the

boys are my true love will be. He's walk - ing down some

197

WILL YOU LOVE ME TOMORROW
(Will You Still Love Me Tomorrow)

Words and Music by GERRY GOFFIN
and CAROLE KING

To-night you're mine com - plete - ly,
Is this a last - ing treas - ure,
I'd like to know that your _____ love

you give your love so sweet - ly,
or just a mo-ment's pleas - ure?
is love I can be sure _____ of.

To -
Can
So

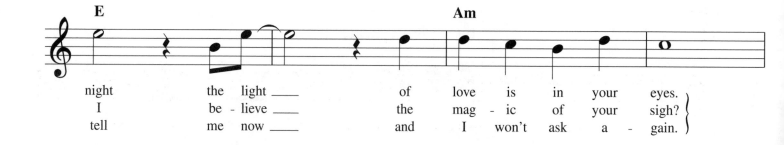

night the light _____ of love is in your eyes.
I be - lieve _____ the mag - ic of your sigh?
tell me now _____ and I won't ask a - gain.

To Coda ⊕

C **G7** **1 C**

Will you still love me to - mor - row?

2

C **F** **Em**

row? To - night with words un - spo - ken,

F **C**

you say that I'm the on - ly one, _____

F **Em**

_____ but will my heart be bro - ken _____

D.S. al Coda

Am **D** **Dm** **G**

_____ when the night _ meets the morn - ing sun? _____

CODA

⊕ **C** **F** **G7** **C**

row? Will you still love me to - mor - row?

YOU TOOK ADVANTAGE OF ME

Words by LORENZ HART
Music by RICHARD RODGERS

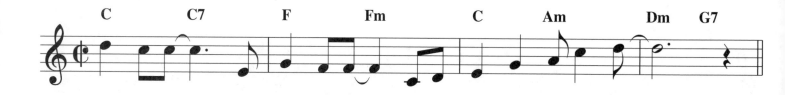

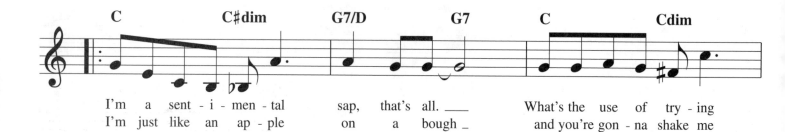

I'm a sent - i - men - tal sap, that's all. ___ What's the use of try - ing
I'm just like an ap - ple on a bough _ and you're gon - na shake me

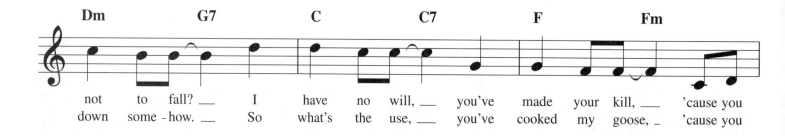

not to fall? ___ I have no will, ___ you've made your kill, ___ 'cause you
down some - how. ___ So what's the use, ___ you've cooked my goose, _ 'cause you

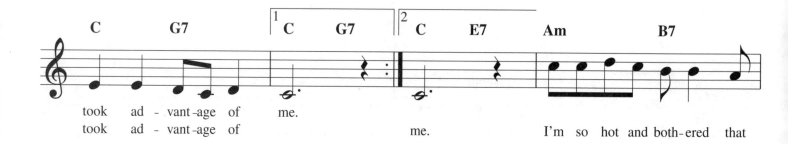

took ad - vant - age of me.
took ad - vant - age of me.
I'm so hot and both - ered that

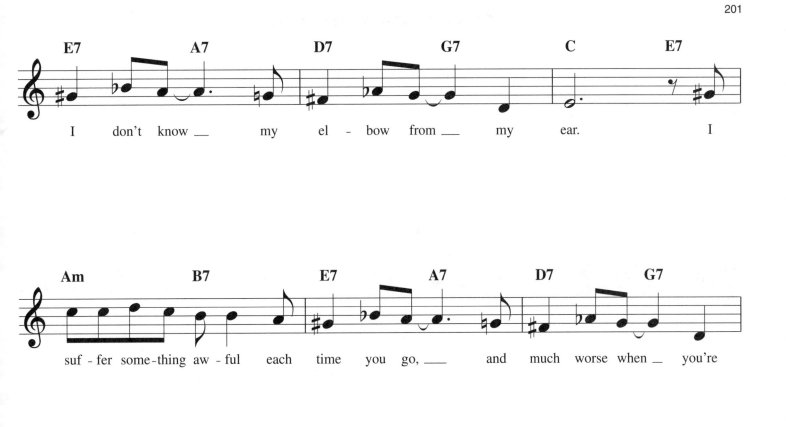

I don't know __ my el - bow from __ my ear. I

suf - fer some-thing aw - ful each time you go, __ and much worse when __ you're

near. Here I am with all my bridg - es burned, __

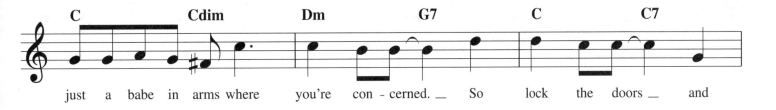

just a babe in arms where you're con - cerned. __ So lock the doors __ and

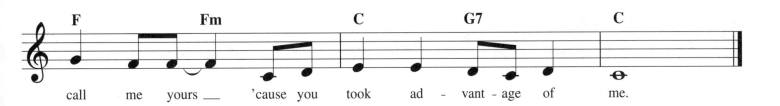

call me yours __ 'cause you took ad - vant - age of me.

YOUR CHEATIN' HEART

Words and Music by
HANK WILLIAMS

Your cheat - in' ___

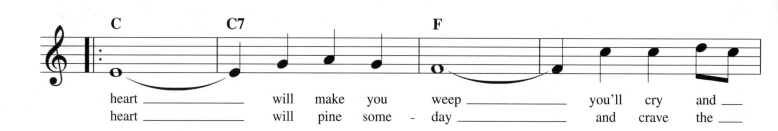

heart _____ will make you weep _____ you'll cry and ___
heart _____ will pine some - day _____ and crave the ___

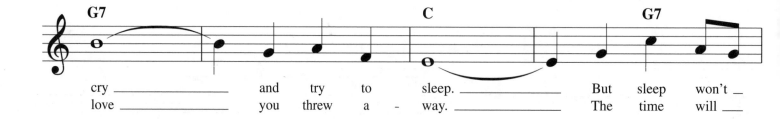

cry _____ and try to sleep. _____ But sleep won't _
love _____ you threw a - way. _____ The time will ___

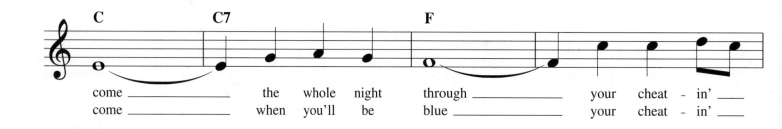

come _____ the whole night through _____ your cheat - in' ___
come _____ when you'll be blue _____ your cheat - in' ___

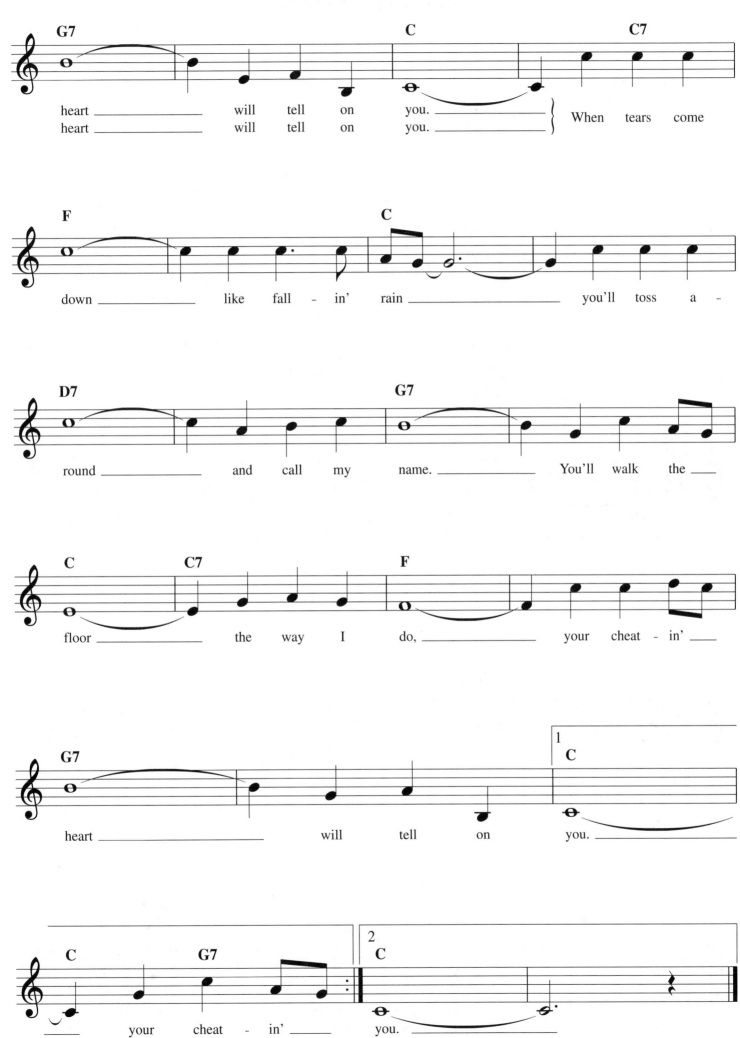

YOU'VE GOT A FRIEND

Words and Music by
CAROLE KING

When you're down _____ and trou - bled, and you need _
_____ a - bove ____ you grows _ dark _

_____ some love and care; ____ and noth -in' _____ noth - in' is go - in' right, _
_____ and full of clouds, __ and that ol' _____ north wind be - gins _ to blow, _

_____ close your eyes __ and think of me, and
_____ keep your head __ to - geth - er, and

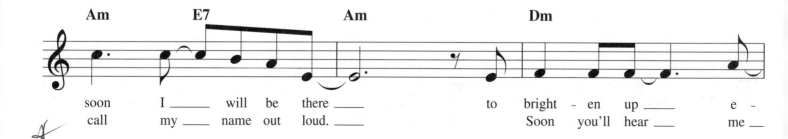

soon I _____ will be there _____ to bright - en up _____ e -
call my ___ name out loud. _____ Soon you'll hear _____ me _

Em   F   G   Dm/G   C

- ven your dark - est night. ____

____ knock-in' at ____ your door. ____

You just call ____ out my ____ name, ____

F   C

____ and you know ____ wher-ev-er I am ____ I'll come run - nin' ____

G7   C

to see you a - gain. ____

Win - ter, spring, sum-mer or fall, ____

C/G   F/A   C/G   C7   To Coda

____ all you have to do is call, _____ and I'll be ____

1.
F   Em   Dm   G7   C   Bm   E7

____ there. _____ You've got a friend. _____ If the sky ____

CHORD SPELLER

C chords

C	C–E–G
Cm	C–E♭–G
C7	C–E–G–B♭
Cdim	C–E♭–G♭
C+	C–E–G#

C# or D♭ chords

C#	C#–F–G#
C#m	C#–E–G#
C#7	C#–F–G#–B
C#dim	C#–E–G
C#+	C#–F–A

D chords

D	D–F#–A
Dm	D–F–A
D7	D–F#–A–C
Ddim	D–F–A♭
D+	D–F#–A#

E♭ chords

E♭	E♭–G–B♭
E♭m	E♭–G♭–B♭
E♭7	E♭–G–B♭–D♭
E♭dim	E♭–G♭–A
E♭+	E♭–G–B

E chords

E	E–G#–B
Em	E–G–B
E7	E–G#–B–D
Edim	E–G–B♭
E+	E–G#–C

F chords

F	F–A–C
Fm	F–A♭–C
F7	F–A–C–E♭
Fdim	F–A♭–B
F+	F–A–C#

F# or G♭ chords

F#	F#–A#–C#
F#m	F#–A–C#
F#7	F#–A#–C#–E
F#dim	F#–A–C
F#+	F#–A#–D

G chords

G	G–B–D
Gm	G–B♭–D
G7	G–B–D–F
Gdim	G–B♭–D♭
G+	G–B–D#

G# or A♭ chords

A♭	A♭–C–E♭
A♭m	A♭–B–E♭
A♭7	A♭–C–E♭–G♭
A♭dim	A♭–B–D
A♭+	A♭–C–E

A chords

A	A–C#–E
Am	A–C–E
A7	A–C#–E–G
Adim	A–C–E♭
A+	A–C#–F

B♭ chords

B♭	B♭–D–F
B♭m	B♭–D♭–F
B♭7	B♭–D–F–A♭
B♭dim	B♭–D♭–E
B♭+	B♭–D–F#

B chords

B	B–D#–F#
Bm	B–D–F#
B7	B–D#–F#–A
Bdim	B–D–F
B+	B–D#–G

Important Note: A slash chord (C/E, G/B) tells you that a certain bass note is to be played under a particular harmony. In the case of C/E, the chord is C and the bass note is E.

HAL LEONARD *presents*

FAKE BOOKS

FOR

BEGINNERS

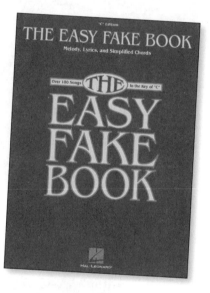

HOW TO PLAY FROM A FAKE BOOK

Faking your own arrangements from
melodies and chords
by Blake Neely

Ever wondered how to create better accompaniments for the melodies in your favorite fake books? This "teach yourself" book introduces you to chord building, various rhythmic styles, and much more, so that you play the songs you like just the way you want them. Keyboard players with a basic understanding of notation and sight-reading will be on their way to more fun with fake books. The relaxed tone of the text and selection of fun songs keep *How to Play From a Fake Book* entertaining throughout – perfect for amateur musicians, or as a supplement for keyboard teachers and their students.

_____00220019 ....$10.95

YOUR FIRST FAKE BOOK

An entry-level fake book! This book features larger-than-most fake book notation with simplified harmonies and melodies – and all songs are in the key of C. An introduction addresses basic instruction in playing from a fake book. Includes over 100 songs, including: Ain't Misbehavin' • All the Things You Are • America the Beautiful • Beauty and the Beast • Bewitched • Blueberry Hill • Can't Help Falling in Love • Don't Get Around Much Anymore • Edelweiss • Getting to Know You • Heart and Soul • It Only Takes a Moment • Leaving on a Jet Plane • Let It Be • Love Me Tender • Maria • Mood Indigo • Satin Doll • Somewhere Out There • Try to Remember • When the Saints Go Marching In • Young at Heart • and more.

_____00240112 ....$19.95

THE EASY FAKE BOOK

This follow-up to the popular *Your First Fake Book* features over 100 more songs for even beginning-level musicians to enjoy. This volume features the same larger notation with simplified harmonies and melodies with all songs in the key of C. In addition, this edition features introductions for each song, adding a more finished sound to the arrangements! Songs include: Alfie • All I Ask of You • Always on My Mind • Angel • Autumn in New York • Blue Skies • Candle in the Wind • Fields of Gold • Grow Old With Me • Hey, Good Lookin' • I'll Be There • Imagine • Memory • Misty • My Heart Will Go On (Love Theme from *Titanic*) • People • Stand by Me • Star Dust • Tears in Heaven • Unchained Melody • What a Wonderful World • and more.

_____00240144 ....$19.95

FOR MORE INFORMATION, SEE YOUR LOCAL MUSIC DEALER,
OR WRITE TO:

HAL•LEONARD®
CORPORATION

7777 W. BLUEMOUND RD. P.O. BOX 13819 MILWAUKEE, WI 53213

Visit Hal Leonard Online at www.halleonard.com

Prices, contents, and availability subject to change without notice